Plough Quarterl

BREAKING GROUND FOR A RENEWED W

Winter 2016, Number 7

Artists: Ferdinand Hodler, Camille Pissarro, Rembrandt, Phillip Gneiting, Fra Angelico, Henry Ossawa Tanner, Fritz von Uhde, Jon Redmond, Balázs Boda, Allan Rohan Crite, Jason Landsel

Cover: A migrant mother and child at a railway station in Salzburg, Austria, wait for a seat on a train to Germany (September 2015). Photograph by Sean Gallup.

Plough Quarterly

BREAKING GROUND FOR A RENEWED WORLD

www.plough.com

Plough Quarterly features original stories, ideas, and culture to inspire everyday faith and action. Starting from the conviction that the teachings and example of Jesus can transform and renew our world, we aim to apply them to all aspects of life, seeking common ground with all people of goodwill regardless of creed. The goal of *Plough Quarterly* is to build a living network of readers, contributors, and practitioners so that, in the words of Hebrews, we may "spur one another on toward love and good deeds."

Plough Quarterly is published by Plough, the publishing house of the Bruderhof, an international movement of Christian communities whose members are called to follow Jesus together in the spirit of the Sermon on the Mount and of the first church in Jerusalem, sharing all talents, income, and possessions (Acts 2 and 4). Bruderhof communities, which include both families and single people from a wide range of backgrounds, are located in the United States, England, Germany, Australia, and Paraguay. Visitors are welcome at any time. To learn more about the Bruderhof's faith, history, and daily life, or to find a community near you to arrange a visit, see *www.bruderhof.com*.

We include contributions in the *Plough Quarterly* which we believe are worthy of our readers' consideration, whether or not we fully agree with them. Views expressed by contributors are their own and do not necessarily reflect the editorial position of Plough or of the Bruderhof communities.

Editors: Peter Mommsen, Sam Hine, Maureen Swinger. Art director: Emily Alexander. Online editor: Erna Albertz. Contributing editors: Veery Huleatt, Charles Moore, Timothy Keiderling, Sung Hoon Park, Raymond Mommsen. Founding Editor: Eberhard Arnold (1883–1935).

Plough Quarterly No. 7: Mercy
Published by Plough Publishing House, ISBN 978-0-87486-745-9
Copyright © 2015 by Plough Publishing House. All rights reserved.

Scripture quotations (unless otherwise noted) are from the New Revised Standard Version Bible, copyright © 1989 the Division of Christian Education of the National Council of the Churches of Christ in the United States of America. Used by permission. All rights reserved.

Front cover: photograph by Sean Gallup / Getty Images. Inside front cover: Ferdinand Hodler, *The Good Samaritan*. Image from WikiArt (public domain). Back cover: Camille Pissarro, *Père Melon Cutting Wood*. Image from WikiArt (public domain).

Editorial Office
PO Box 398
Walden, NY 12586
T: 845.572.3455
info@plough.com

Subscriber Services
PO Box 345
Congers, NY 10920-0345
T: 800.521.8011
subscriptions@plough.com

United Kingdom
Brightling Road
Robertsbridge
TN32 5DR
T: +44(0)1580.883.344

Australia
4188 Gwydir Highway
Elsmore, NSW
2360 Australia
T: +61(0)2.6723.2213

Plough Quarterly (ISSN 2372-2584) is published quarterly by Plough Publishing House, PO Box 398, Walden, NY 12586. Individual subscription $32 per year in the United States; Canada add $8, other countries add $16. Periodicals postage paid at Walden, NY 12586 and at additional mailing offices.
POSTMASTER: Send address changes to *Plough Quarterly*, PO Box 345, Congers, NY 10920-0345.

Dear Reader,

It's rare for a national leader to court political risk in order to help strangers. Yet that's what Angela Merkel, chancellor of Germany, did in September when she opened her country's borders to refugees from the Middle East, especially Syria.

Merkel's actions weren't purely selfless, of course, but based in part on political and national interests. And German cities and villages must now house up to 1.5 million newcomers by year's end, sorely testing the public's acceptance and goodwill. All the same, this was a brave decision carrying real moral clarity. It showed the world what mercy looks like.

"Blessed are the merciful, for they shall obtain mercy." Jesus' words cut through our excuses, mixed motives, and timidities. Of course, caution has its place; many public policy questions are complicated. What's not complicated is the desperation of families fleeing terror in Syria, Iraq, and Afghanistan (see page 22). In cases like these, mercy is easy to recognize – as is the lack of it.

What would it look like if the United States followed Germany's lead and offered mercy to the throngs of Central Americans, many fleeing horrific violence, who seek to cross our southern border? No doubt this would involve risk, expense, and disruption to our way of life. Yet Jesus' words hardly leave Christians the choice of looking away. (See Tolstoy's story on page 55.) Couldn't the challenge of mercy draw out what is noblest in our traditions and in our youth?

Mercy, surely, doesn't stop there. To take a few examples, what does mercy look like in relation to the 2.2 million people being held in US prisons and jails? Or the working poor unable to adequately care for their families? Or the millions of children paying the bitter price of the sexual revolution and its erosion of lifelong marriage between a child's father and mother?

Pope Francis, who has brought many of these concerns to the world's attention, has announced a Jubilee Year of Mercy starting December 8, 2015: "We are called to show mercy because mercy has first been shown to us. Pardoning offences becomes the clearest expression of merciful love, and for us Christians it is an imperative from which we cannot excuse ourselves."

Nowhere is mercy more concrete than in the act of forgiving, as shown by stories from North Korea, New York, and Auschwitz (pages 10, 28, and 38). Is there anything that cannot be forgiven? That's the question that Hanna-Barbara Gerl-Falkovitz grapples with in her essay on page 36.

God's limitless mercy showed itself in flesh and blood in the birth of Jesus (page 45). In all we do in 2016, may we make his priorities our own. To our readers who have encouraged us and pointed us in this direction over the past year, our sincere thanks.

Warm greetings,

Peter

Peter Mommsen
Editor

3

Octavian Smigelschi, Young Man Reading

Loving the Terrorist

On Peggy Gish's "Learning to Love Boko Haram," Autumn 2015: The reconciliation work being done by the EYN church in Nigeria is remarkable – if only we would see more such positive stories published! The article reminds us that not all Boko Haram members are monsters: they too are children of God and fellow human beings. How do we know how we would act in their place if swept along by extremes of fear, injustice, religious zeal, and anger? The path toward reconciliation, as EYN pastor Markus Gamache says in Gish's article, starts with listening to other people's problems.

June Curtis

In September 2014, more than 120 Islamic scholars denounced ISIS, with which Boko Haram is allied, not only for being un-Islamic, but also for being against all humankind.

Who are we to forgive what was done to the orphans who lost their fathers to these gangs? How could we love the terrorists while mothers are sobbing for their loved ones? How could we love those who have destroyed the homes and the livelihood of people? God will not allow such people into his paradise.

Love those who are loved by Jesus and God. Dislike those who are disliked by Jesus and God, so that truth and falsehood will become clear.

Abu Nahidian, Manassas Mosque

I had a good discussion with a brother here [in prison] who loves your magazine but refused to even read Gish's article. I told him we should start by praying for our parole board! Gish's article reminds me of why I love Donald Kraybill's book *The Upside-Down Kingdom:* Jesus' message was the opposite of the culture and religion of his time.

Don Mason

Syria's Children

On Cat Carter's "The Children of War," Summer 2015: It is hard to read such stories without wanting to scream in rage and sorrow. It is hard for me to relate to such pain and such acts of degradation. I keep on wondering why the whole world doesn't stop until this violence is put to an end.

The hardest challenge of pacifism (and I speak very personally here) is first to learn to discern the truth of the situation, and then to be willing to give one's life as others have rather than to resort to violence. This poor world is in dire need of a great movement of the Holy Spirit which will change hearts from greed to giving, from hate to love, and from seeing others as tools for profit to seeing them as brothers and sisters.

Edward A. Hara

The Meaning of Marriage

On "No Time for Silence" (editorial), N. T. Wright's "What Is Marriage For?," and John Huleatt's "After Obergefell," *Autumn 2015:* I admire both the spirit and content of John Huleatt's essay on the possibilities of Christian witness for marriage in the wake of the

---

We welcome letters to the editor. Letters and web comments may be edited for length and clarity, and may be published in any medium. Letters should be sent with the writer's name and address to letters@plough.com.

Rick Warren and Jacqueline Rivers were among the speakers introducing the new Plough title *Not Just Good, but Beautiful.*

Obergefell v. Hodges Supreme Court decision legalizing same-sex marriage nationwide. As someone who publicly opposed gay marriage for a long time before changing my view in 2012, I respond favorably to Huleatt's suggestion in the essay that, while he firmly opposes gay marriage, he also recognizes that both sides have worthy claims and that each side therefore deserves respect from the other and from the larger society. This argument is not common. In my experience, almost all partisans on either side of this debate have argued that the struggle is an all-or-nothing contest between good (their side) and evil (the other side). Huleatt's fresher approach is more generous and more hopeful – and also, I think, more faithful to the facts. I also strongly agree with his insistence that the church "must never stop engaging the world" and that now "the church is free to focus on what matters most."

David Blankenhorn
Institute for American Values

I have found some articles in the past two issues to be bordering on homophobic and bigoted. Marriage is a civil union, not a religious one. People who choose to do so may continue to have a religious ceremony. The new ruling by the Supreme Court only allows same-sex couples to be legally married and those marriages to be legally recognized and binding in all fifty states. To deny this is discriminatory and now illegal. *Allen King*

As a Christian in the United Kingdom who has stepped out of church leadership as a result of the same-sex partnership issue – I'm an exploring "agnostic" who believes there should be respect for a diversity of viewpoints in the church – I am puzzled by some items in the Autumn 2015 *Plough*.

These articles seem to conflate the larger issue of marriage with the narrower issue

Celebrating Marriage

Philadelphia, September 24, 2015

To mark the release of a book of essays by Pope Francis and diverse religious leaders and scholars titled *Not Just Good, but Beautiful: The Complementary Relationship between Man and Woman,* Plough hosted an interfaith panel at Philadelphia's National Museum of American Jewish History during the World Meeting of Families.

As Dr. Jacqueline C. Rivers, director of the Seymour Institute for Black Church and Policy Studies, told the audience: "Our concern for the family is about the poor. Men and women suffer from the retreat from marriage, which is now common among the poor, but even more so among the black community. And it's the innocent who suffer most – the children."

Pastor Rick Warren, author of *The Purpose Driven Life* and another contributor to the book, added: "I think we need to celebrate good marriages. I think we need to celebrate strong families – rather than being an opponent of the negative, being a proponent of what's right. . . . We came to this conference from a lot of different perspectives, but there was one thing we agreed on: you can't have a strong nation, a strong community, a strong congregation without strong families."

A Jewish perspective was offered by Daniel Mark, a professor at Villanova. Other speakers included D. Todd Christofferson, a Mormon leader; Helen Alvaré from the George Mason School of Law; and Gerhard Cardinal Müller from the Vatican. Watch their talks at *plough.com/events.*

of same-sex marriage, with some confusing detours into remarriage after divorce. Tom Wright's article (I'm a fan of his) on the creation narrative, the biblical imagery of marriage, and remarriage after divorce touches only tangentially on same-sex partnerships.

Most confusing of all is the statement taken from *Foundations of Our Faith and Calling,* which you declare to be "a simple reminder of what scripture teaches." Here, you confuse Jesus' teaching on divorce with teaching on

Engels Kozlov, *Blue Herring*

same-sex partnerships (about which Jesus says nothing). You do not mention Matthew's concession for remarriage after divorce (Matt. 19:9), nor Paul's exception (1 Cor. 7:15). You have not provided the "simple reminder of what scripture teaches," but rather a considerably edited interpretation.

Much clearer thinking is needed than this. The church needs to listen to those whose behavior it proscribes in relation to same-sex partnerships. There is too much grandstanding, and too little listening.

This is why I read carefully Bruderhof teaching as reflected in *Plough.* Although I am not an Anabaptist by tradition, I continue to find much that I am learning from and seeking to apply in my life. *Peter Wilkinson*

As a seventy-eight-year-old man blessed with six children and eleven grandchildren, I was moved by your courageous exposition of what Christian marriage really means. Now more than ever, Christians need to stand firm and state their case in the face of increasing cynicism and hostility. You did that with love and conviction. Thank you. *Tony Lazenby*

Christian Nonviolence, Continued

On Tom Cornell's "The Future of Christian Nonviolence," Summer 2015: I know Tom and appreciate his valuable insights, borne of a lifelong commitment to gospel peacemaking. But as a participant in two Plowshares actions, I offer the following thoughts on his essay:

The basic hope of any Plowshares action is to communicate a faith that the power of nonviolent love can overcome the forces of violence; a reverence for the sacredness of all life and creation; a plea for the victims of poverty and the arms race; an acceptance of personal responsibility for the dismantling and the physical conversion of the weapons; and a spiritual conversion of the heart to the way of justice and reconciliation. This hope should guide us from the moment of entering a weapons plant or military base, and throughout the subsequent court process and prison witness.

I view Plowshares actions as symbolic and, ultimately, as experiments in truth. The intent of such actions is to uphold God's law, and international laws which prohibit the possession and use of weapons of indiscriminate mass destruction – weapons that imperil all of God's creation. For me, the actions I participated in were a form of intercessory prayer, aimed at personal and societal conversion and transformation. *Art Laffin*
Catholic Worker, Washington, DC

MICHAEL MANNING

The Gospel at the Margins

WHEN BOBBY showed up at Graih's drop-in center in Douglas, the small town that is the Isle of Man's capital, he had lost almost everything to alcoholism: his job, his house, his marriage. Now drink was threatening to take from him the last dregs of his mental and physical health.

The drop-in, which provides free food and emergency accommodation, was not a place Bobby (names have been changed) wanted to go. He saw himself as better than the drug-ravaged addicts that he knew gathered there. But now he was desperate.

Simply to live on the Isle of Man – an isolated splinter of land in the Irish Sea between Great Britain and Ireland, home to some eighty-five thousand souls – is to exist on the margins. As a British Crown dependency, the island has become an offshore banking haven. Those like Bobby who don't benefit from the local financial and tourist industries find themselves doubly sidelined. It's for them that Graih exists.

Here at Graih – the word means *love* in Manx, the island's Gaelic language – we serve the homeless and those in insecure accommodation. Our focus is meeting practical needs and building up relationships. Many of our volunteers are not Christians, yet again and again, as we share food around our dining table, curiosity is evoked: Why are you like this? What's different?

Those are the questions Bobby asked when he reluctantly arrived at the drop-in. As he told us later, it wasn't so much what the people who served him said, but rather what he described as the "joy" and "freedom" they had. The desire to find the same for himself became a thirst that eventually proved more powerful than his thirst for alcohol.

Bobby began to recall a faith he had abandoned in childhood. The relationships he formed led him to church services and baptism. To his surprise, he began to make headway in his battle against alcoholism. With this freedom came a new way of life as Bobby began to pray and help others who struggled.

I GREW UP in a tradition where the gospel started with an oft-repeated assertion that I was a hopeless sinner. I needed a Savior – Jesus – and all I had to do was to accept him as my Lord.

Michael Manning is a coordinator with Graih, a charity based on the Isle of Man, and is the author of No King but God: Walking as Jesus Walked *(Resource Publications, 2015).* www.graih.org.im

But the men at Graih don't need to be told they are sinners. They have already been told they're failures by a host of others: family, friends, the courts, even themselves. Nor do they need to be reminded that something's wrong. There is Trevor, unable to function without copious amounts of pre-scribed and illegal drugs; Brian, wrapped up in the memory of his children's deaths; Malcolm, carrying the insecurity of a childhood of rejection, adoption, and bullying; and Ross, who slept in a car park following a mental breakdown.

These guys have been around all the programs and have had their fill of quick fixes, easy answers, admonitions, and promises. "Accept Jesus as your Lord and Savior." What does that even mean?

People dwelling in darkness need light. The gospel doesn't come into situations of pain and need as an exposition of brokenness but rather as sheer practical good news: the invitation to follow a different king.

I first became involved with the drop-in as an eighteen-year-old who knew nothing about substance abuse or mental health. A friend of mine had recently returned from experiencing extreme poverty abroad, and he was passion-ate about getting to work on the island. I was terrified, but also unable to refuse to join him: I couldn't identify myself as a Christian and yet be unwilling to meet with broken people. Wasn't Jesus castigated for spending time with the unclean, those eking out an existence on the underbelly of society (Mark 2:15–17)? Didn't he say clearly that following him means living as the "poor" (Luke 6:20–26)?

We started by offering food, then emergency accommodation as well. It was uncomfortable to know that we could return to our warm beds while others had nowhere to go. Some of our volunteers began to offer radical hospitality, taking people in off the streets and giving them a sense of home. Although the risks were great for both hosts and guests, the fruit was bountiful.

I soon realized that without time spent around the table at the Graih drop-in, my faith would become impoverished and sterile. To have people of different ages, races, backgrounds, and levels of wealth come together to share food as equals has always been one of the most subversive aspects of the church – and one of the most humorous.

I now live with my wife and two young sons in a shared household, seeking to live a common life and to stay open to those on the margins. Part of Graih's vision is a com-munity house where hospitality and a sense of belonging can be offered to the homeless, those leaving prison, or those suffering from mental illness. Over the years God's faithfulness has encouraged us to take small steps toward his kingdom, and we continue to yearn for oppor-tunities to embody more of what that kingdom looks like.

We want our proclamation of the gospel to be an invitation into true humanity. The way we live every day, the company we keep, and the relationships we foster proclaim more than the words we speak.

Perhaps this shouldn't surprise us, as people of the King who took the form of a slave to dwell among us – who broke bread and shared wine, who fed the hungry and liberated the captive, who took the weight of a sin-sick world to the cross, and who trod gentle steps of hope in a garden on Easter morning. The gospel indeed. ➤

Our Daily Bread

"Does God make the bread you get from the store?" My daughter's question baffled me until I remembered how several evenings earlier our family had read the Lord's Prayer together. She hadn't said anything at the time, but she must have taken the words "Give us this day our daily bread" literally.

And why shouldn't we pray for literal bread? Trading money for a sliced, wrapped, and labeled product doesn't take me into the mystery of the Maker. That amazement was reserved for the first time I teetered on a chair at my mother's elbow, pummeling and shaping loaves, marveling at the sharp scent, the cycle of action and rest, and the sunny window that seemed to magically double the quantity of dough. Try explaining the puzzle of yeast to a six-year-old – for example, the one who now teeters at my elbow. "Well," she says after I've tried several times, "at least God knows how it works." Someday, she and I will go look up the science. But probably not before the next row of loaves is cooling on the counter. For now, something about their realness points us back to God, by way of the wheat field.

There are other harvests. In the Genesis creation story, all the creatures that moved on the ground were "very good" in God's sight. And that goodness is not only to delight the eye of the beholder, as our family learned during one of those interminable northeastern winters that really needs a mother to remind it that it's just one of *four* seasons. Food prices were up, and we had five mouths to feed. When my husband took his bow out into the gray cold and returned with a buck that packed sixty-four pounds of meat, the children discovered a new respect for hard-won food claimed from the forest, not the store.

When it was time to make venison sausage, they were underfoot throughout, with noses almost contributively close to the meat grinder. They cackled at the sausage casings twitching about in the rinsing water. They stirred spices, sending up plumes of sage and pepper.

I'm glad they know that the roast on the table is venison back strap. They should know how to prepare meat, how to spice and serve and share it with others. But after dinner, with the dark gathered close around the house and the wind leaning on the windows, our daughter looked out to the treeline and remembered an earlier season, when we watched a doe and her fawns drifting along the edge of a summer dusk with fireflies weaving all around them, as misty as the fawns' flecks in the last of the light. The same God who provided us with food and the ability to harvest it gave us also these moments of breath-catching beauty – bread for the soul. ⤳

Maureen Swinger

KIM HYUN-SIK

Forgiving Kim Jong-il

Kim Jong-il's funeral procession in 2011 in Pyongyang, North Korea

I am now more than eighty years old, and already twenty-five years have passed since I left Pyongyang. Ever since the Korean War, when I barely survived the intense fighting against American troops, my life has felt precarious. All I want now is to see the people of North Korea living free and in the love of Jesus, even if only for one day. This is my story.

Sunday School

My mother had eight children in all, but lost two sons to measles. Early on Sunday morning she would wake me – just me, the youngest – and wash me with water heated in the kettle, dress me in fresh clothes, and trim my fingernails and toenails. Then she would get ashes from the kitchen fireplace and polish the coins for the church collection until they shone before putting them in my pocket. She would tell me to stand straight and sing the Sunday school song loudly. I can still remember the words:

> Through another week
> God has protected us in our weakness.
> On this happy day, beloved friend,
> I gladly take your hand.
> Let us praise God's grace,
> Let us study God's word.

My mother's name was Lee Geum-nyo, which means "silken woman." Like her name, she was as tender and good as silk. She was a skilled seamstress and made clothes for everyone in the neighborhood. Whenever people needed

Kim Hyun-sik was the tutor of Kim Jong-il, ruler of North Korea from 1994 to 2011. Since coming to the United States in 2003, the author has taught as a visiting professor at Yale University and as a research professor at George Mason University, and has lectured widely on North Korea.

Photograph from KCNA

clothing made from materials that are hard to work with such as silk or ramie, the work would fall to her.

From about the time I was old enough to be aware, my mother suffered from chronic illness (cancer, as it turned out). One biting cold winter night – I was fourteen – she looked at her children one after another. Then she suddenly embraced me and prayed, "Father God, why are you taking me away so soon? How can I leave these young ones? Please watch over my children. Please let my youngest son become a pastor." While she prayed, her hot tears fell on my cheeks. That night my mother died. She was forty-five years old.

War

Two years later, early in the morning of June 25, 1950, we awoke to the news that there would be a special broadcast by Kim Il-sung, the leader of North Korea. As he spoke, his characteristically hoarse voice was filled with agitation:

Early this morning, the South Korean puppet army crossed the thirty-eighth parallel in a surprise invasion of our country. Our valiant People's Army drove them back over the border and is pressing southward. I call on all citizens to rise as one in this holy war to drive back the puppet army. Victory will be ours.

I had just finished eleventh grade. From that day on, in every school and workplace, people were exhorted to join the army, and every day there were induction ceremonies. In my high school, the entire student body joined the army as soon as our physical examinations were done. I joined the newly formed North Hamgyong Marine Corps and was sent directly into combat.

Five months later, after a day of fighting through snow-covered hills, I took shelter in an isolated house at the foot of a mountain. My cotton boots were frozen through. The old woman who lived there built a fire for me and gave me some bean cake. While I was gulping

The author with his mother and family on his first birthday, 1933

it down, she studied me carefully and finally said, "You're from a Christian family, aren't you, little soldier?"

At that time, Christians were subject to heavy surveillance and persecution. Her question shocked me.

"What makes you say that, Grandmother?"

"It's in your face. You can't fool an old deaconess."

Suddenly I poured out my whole story to her – how I had believed in Jesus from my earliest days, how I lost my mother when I was fourteen, and how, as she was dying, she had begged me to become a pastor.

When I finished, she grabbed my hand and said, "Beloved son, let us pray: Lord, please do not let this boy soldier die on this terrible battlefield. He must fulfill his mother's last wish and become a pastor. Please protect him. Let him live to do work that is pleasing to you."

As soon as it grew light, the shooting began again. That morning during a fierce firefight, I was hit by shrapnel in my head and legs. My last thought before losing consciousness was wondering why hot sticky water was flowing from my head.

When I woke up, I wasn't on the battlefield anymore. My head and legs were tightly bandaged, and all around me were wounded soldiers. I felt intense pain in my head, and when I reached up to feel it, I found a scrap of paper had been placed next to me. It read:

> I used to live next door to you before I went to medical school. Now I'm a nurse in the People's Army. I hope I can save your life by putting you on a train to China. You need to survive. I'll see you back at home.
>
> Choi Suk-jong, December 3, 1950

The soldier in the next bed had been watching me all this time. "I'm glad you finally woke up," he said. "You were unconscious for so long I was wondering if you'd died on us."

"Where am I?"

"In the army hospital in Changchun, China. They brought you in ten days ago. The UN did a big bombing raid that day and lots of casualties came in. They only sent back the ones who were likely to survive with treatment. They buried the rest in a big hole with the dead. When they checked your ID card to report you killed in action, Choi Suk-jong found out who you were and made them put you on the train. They said they couldn't take soldiers who were as good as dead, but she told them you were her younger brother, and begged the commanding officer until he let her put you in the cargo compartment. She even

Photograph courtesy of Kim Hyun-sik

tied you in place with twine so you wouldn't fall out, and put a diaper on you. You'd be dead if it wasn't for her."

I remembered Choi Suk-jong – she was in the choir at our old church. When the war was over, I looked everywhere for her, but no one knew where she was. Later I learned that the day after I was transported, a bombing raid killed nearly everyone in the field hospital.

The following July, I was discharged from the army because of my disability – I still had shrapnel in my head close to the brain, though this was only discovered by a surgeon twenty-five years later. I heard that in North Korea Kim Il-sung had reopened the colleges and was recruiting students, so I and two others received recommendations and departed for Pyongyang, the North Korean capital.

Once over the border, we rode on the back of a truck through Pyongyang province. Suddenly we were hit by a bombing attack. We were thrown high into the air and crashed back to earth. I woke up feeling cold all over, and found that I had gone headfirst into a rice paddy. The truck was blown to pieces. One of the men was dead, his head smashed on a rock by the roadside. The other had simply disappeared – he was never found.

Alone now, I dragged myself along until I arrived at Pyongyang two weeks later. There I found the Department of Education in an underground bomb shelter in the Moranbong area. A man who looked like a Party cadre welcomed me. A Russian-born Korean, he had been sent by Stalin to help rebuild Korea after the Japanese occupation ended. When he found that I'd studied Russian in high school, he enrolled me in the Teachers' College as a Russian major and he became my mentor, tutoring me in Russian. After I graduated, he recommended me for a professorship.

My Student, Kim Jong-il

I had married and was a professor when I first met Kim Jong-il. Today he is remembered as a cruel dictator, but when I first met him in 1959, he was a shy young man with fluffy hair and cheeks that turned bright red when he was embarrassed. His father, Kim Il-sung, told me to test him in Russian, since he said that his ability in that language was wretched. (Kim Il-sung had fought in the Soviet army and so was fluent in Russian.) I called the boy to the principal's office, where I administered an oral examination.

Fifty years later, I can still remember the sentences that I asked Kim Jong-il to translate into Russian: "I love and respect my father. After I graduate high school, I plan to enter Kim Il-sung University. I enjoy movies more than sports."

As he struggled to answer my questions, his cheeks turned crimson and his brow beaded with sweat. He seemed very young and innocent, not the least bit arrogant or conceited that he was Kim Il-sung's son.

After the examination, Kim Il-sung ordered me to give his son private instruction in conversational Russian. Our lessons continued for the next year, and the young man worked hard. Each day when the session was over, he would walk with me to the door and slip Russian chocolate or Chinese cigarettes into my pocket. After I told him that I didn't smoke, he gave me Chinese candies instead.

His "graduation" took place at a Russian cultural evening during the National Conference of Russian Teachers. Kim Jong-il recited Pushkin's poem, "Winter Road." His recitation was beautiful and well-timed: outside a violent snowstorm was blowing. The audience cheered deafeningly, shouting his Russian name: "Kim Yura, Kim Yura!" He ran over to me, embraced

Photograph courtesy of Kim Hyun-sik

me, and burst into tears. I was so proud of him that I wept also.

The last time I met Kim Jong-il was twenty years later. It was in 1978, at the celebration of the thirtieth anniversary of North Korea's establishment. I, together with the foreign vice-minister, was on the premier's platform in Kim Il-sung Square, preparing to receive the Chinese premier. Late that night, Kim Jong-il appeared on the platform and spoke with me shortly. As he left, he seized my hand, shook it powerfully, and said, "Let's meet again. We need to see each other again."

Moscow

When Seoul won its bid to host the 1988 Olympics, the world's awareness of both South and North Korea shot up. The Soviet Union had long sponsored North Korea's Communist regime, but now began taking the relationship more seriously. Soviet universities began opening Korean language departments. As they did not have enough qualified Korean instructors, Soviet academics flooded into Pyongyang to learn Korean. I was one of the few qualified North Korean professors, so much of the work fell to me.

By that time, I had decades of language-teaching experience and knew many tricks to make it engaging. The Russians enjoyed my classes and studied industriously. Soon, however, they began to complain about the shabby classrooms and uncomfortable apartments, and demanded that I be sent to Russia to teach them Korean there. Surprisingly enough, the Party agreed, and in 1988 I was sent to Moscow as an exchange professor.

Word soon spread among students that the new Korean professor's classes were easy and effective. After about two months, South Korean intelligence agents also heard about my classes and got in contact with me. They suggested that I defect from North to South

Korea, but I refused. After so many years as a professor in North Korea, including a role as private tutor for Kim Il-sung's relatives, I had no interest in leaving my family behind.

When I rejected their offers, the South Korean agents tracked down my older sister, whom I had heard nothing of for years. During the war, she had escaped to South Korea on a US Navy ship and finally settled in Chicago; I had despaired of ever seeing her again. Now the South Korean agents made arrangements for us to meet. Her sudden arrival in Moscow in November 1991 began a chain of events that threw my life into confusion.

She was now seventy years old. When I took her hand and thought of the hard journey she'd made to see me in the bitter winter, I burst into tears. She stayed for a week, and our times together were mostly spent crying. In the meantime I tried to keep up appearances, arriving punctually at the university every day, and being careful not to let on that anything was out of the ordinary.

The day after she returned to America, I received an urgent message from North Korean intelligence ordering me to leave Russia the next day and return to Pyongyang. I would later learn that the Russian–South Korean contact who guided my sister was a double agent. He had told the North Koreans everything we did, what we said, and even what we ate during our week together.

Decision

What should I do? I knew that if I went back to North Korea as ordered, the best I could hope for would be to lose everything I'd worked for and be sent to a political prison camp. More likely, I would face the firing squad. "Why did you meet with an enemy national? How long have you been in contact with South Korean spies?" They would torture me and frame me for all manner of crimes.

What would make my sentence even more severe was the fact that I had hidden my sister's existence from the authorities for forty years. The North Korean government still viewed the United States as the enemy, and if they had known I had a relative living there, I would have been treated as a person of suspicious character and barred from attending university or living in Pyongyang. Apart from the charge of espionage, they could now also prove that I had falsified my family records to hide my sister's existence.

I went back and forth in my mind. If I defected, my family would be in danger, as would the colleagues who had given me character references. Yet on the other hand, I knew that even if I went back to face punishment, they were already in danger anyway.

An added complication was the global political situation. Just then, in the last weeks of 1991, the Soviet Union was disintegrating, making North Korea's position precarious. In Europe, the communist governments were falling one after another; in Romania, Kim Il-sung's close friend, the dictator Nicolae Ceaușescu, had been shot. Meanwhile the formerly divided countries of Germany, Vietnam, and Yemen were now reunited, and it seemed likely that in North Korea too, Kim Il-sung's regime would soon collapse, allowing the reunification of my country. South Korean agents counseled me that if I defected, I could wait in safety until that happened, and then return to my family.

I had twenty-four hours to make this excruciating decision. I thought of my wife in Pyongyang, of how she wept when I left for Russia and told me to come back safely.

My beloved wife. She and I had met in college and married in 1955, when Pyongyang was a city of rubble. She supported me when I was physically and mentally broken by the war. Together we had had two sons and two daughters. We had experienced loss as well: our youngest son, Hunchol, had died of brain cancer before graduating from college. But the other children had grown up healthy, and we had been a happy, contented family. Now we had five grandchildren.

When I traveled to Russia, my wife had written in my notebook in large letters: "Shoes, fabric and cotton to make quilts, reading glasses." These items were hard to come by in North Korea, and she wanted to be sure I remembered to buy them in Russia. The reading glasses were for her, the shoes were for the grandchildren, and the fabric was to make a quilt for our youngest daughter. I had bought all the gifts as soon as I received my first paycheck in Russia.

What would happen now to my grandchildren? I remembered how, before my departure, they had laughed in anticipation as they traced around their feet on sheets of paper so that Grandpa could buy the right size . . .

I didn't sleep that night. I kept seeing the faces of my family and my students. Finally I decided to go south.

In disguise at a Russian port, ready to board a ship to South Korea, 1992

The next day, instead of going to work, I went to a safe house prepared by South Korean intelligence – my life underground had begun. As soon as I disappeared, the Russian and the North Korean intelligence services began a frantic hunt for me, blockading all shipyards and airports.

The South Korean safe house was just next door to the North Korean embassy. Outside my hiding place, the streets were crawling with agents. But, as the saying goes, "It's darkest under the lamp": they never dreamed I was hiding under their noses. After six months, the North Koreans gave up the search, and the South Korean agents spread rumors that I had been disappeared by the Russian mafia.

The South Koreans gave me the passport of a Russian-Korean and disguised me to resemble his photograph. In June 1992, I was put on a plane to the west coast of Russia, then placed on a ship bound for South Korea. Before leaving the shipyard, Russian security agents searched the vessel for smuggled goods and stowaways. The boat's owner told me to climb to the top of the funnel and hide in a narrow crawlspace, where I remained for five hours until the agents had left. When I came out, I was barely alive – my face was black with smoke and ash and covered with tears.

I was lying on my narrow bunk when I finally felt the ship begin to move. Now I knew I would never return home. My family's faces came to me one after another and tormented me until I thought I'd lose my mind. Why had I chosen this way? Surely it would have been better to return and all go to prison camp together. My heart was full of agony.

After two days, the ship docked at Masan, South Korea.

Hunger Strike

When I disembarked in South Korea, intelligence agents met me, and as soon as we boarded the train for Seoul they began interrogating me.

"Why did you come here?"

Why did I come here? You called my sister all the way from America. You made it impossible for me to go back to Pyongyang. You told me that if I defected, my family would be safe.

"Did you commit a serious crime in North Korea? Was it because of money problems? Did you say something reactionary?"

I had a sense of foreboding, but did not worry greatly. Maybe, I thought, they hadn't heard about the nature of my escape, and everything would be cleared up once I got to Seoul. But on arriving there, I was taken to a secret prison where the interrogation continued.

"You need to release your identity to the press. Who are these pupils of yours who guaranteed your character?"

I was dumbfounded. I had defected on the condition that my identity would be kept

BUSINESS REPLY MAIL
FIRST–CLASS MAIL   PERMIT NO. 332   CONGERS, NY

POSTAGE WILL BE PAID BY ADDRESSEE

PLOUGH QUARTERLY
PO BOX 345
CONGERS NY 10920–9895

secret – it was the only thing I could do to limit the damage to those I left behind. And now, the minute I arrived in South Korea, they disregarded their promise. Every day they asked the same question over and over again:

"Why did you come?"

Now I had to ask myself this question. Why had I risked my life to come to Seoul? My time in Russia with my sister, her tears and prayers, were a distant memory.

I eventually answered: "Well, it seems now that I shouldn't have come here. Your agents brought me here: if there's anything you don't know about me, I don't know it either. As of now, I'm going on a hunger strike. I have nothing further to say to you or to hear from you. If I die here quietly, at least it won't be too bad for my family and pupils."

Once I had set my mind, I wasn't even hungry when they brought my food. After a week, my mind grew hazy. It seemed better to die than to continue this craven existence. Finally, when I was close to death, the agents gave in. I broke my fast only after getting their firm promise not to leak my name to the press. This was two weeks after I had stopped eating.

Starting Over

I erased the fifty years I had lived in North Korea, and began a new existence with a new name. My old self died with my name and was buried forever in my memory, but nothing was easy about adapting to the new society. Every day I asked myself why I had come. I despaired of the new life I had chosen. What should I do in this bewildering country? More than anything, I was filled with resentment against the people who had gone through the trouble of getting my sister from America to get me here. I was disgusted with myself for putting myself in their hands. My regrets and bitterness kept me awake many nights.

Months passed. Then, one day, I heard that Kim Jong-il, my old student, had ordered all my family shot.

The news of their deaths ripped my heart. Their faces hung before my eyes: the wife who had shared my life, the sons and daughters we had raised, our daughter-in-law, our five sweet grandchildren . . .

I could not forgive myself for my part in their deaths. My hunger strike to hide my identity had all been wasted effort. I lost all desire for life. Many times I resolved to kill myself. Whenever I thought of Kim Jong-il, bitterness and rage surged through me. Hatred was all I had left.

For a long time I struggled to find my place in South Korea – I was constantly afraid for my safety, and unaccustomed to this new way of life with so many choices. Eventually, I found help from Kim Hyun-ja, a woman whom I had first met in Russia. We became better acquainted and in 1994 we married. In 2003 we moved to the United States.

Soon universities asked me to lecture on North Korea, and I began to put more and more effort into the work of reunification. Every morning, my wife and I read in the Bible and prayed together.

One day I prayed: "Lord God, Kim Jong-il has starved hundreds of thousands of my countrymen to death and made my homeland into a living hell. For his own power, he had my whole family shot, yet he lives on without shame. Let lightning strike him and bring him to judgment. I pray in the name of Jesus, Amen!"

My wife said, "I can't say 'Amen' to that prayer. I believe God loves even Kim Jong-il."

"You may believe as you wish. Isn't God a God of justice? If so, should he not judge Kim Jong-il?"

The author with his second wife, Kim Hyun-ja

"Yes, he is a God of justice, but he is also a God of love. You must forgive Kim Jong-il." So on that day, we each said "Amen" to our own prayers. This disagreement between us lasted for an entire year.

The change came one day when we were reading the Book of Exodus together. I was struck by the words: "God hardened Pharaoh's heart." Perhaps, I thought, God uses people like Pharaoh – people like Kim Jong-il – for his own purposes.

It was then that I knew I had to forgive him. It took a hard struggle to do so. But when I overcame and was able to forgive Kim Jong-il, a great peace came into my heart. After that, my wife and I could pray together again. Every day we prayed for him.

As a result, in 2007 I decided to write him a letter. Here it is in part:

Dear Chairman Kim,

It's now twenty-eight years since I last spoke with you in Kim Il-sung Square. Since then, I have changed, you have changed, the world has changed.

After leaving Pyongyang, I lived ten years in Seoul, and now am living in the land of the "eternal foe," America. I can't cover all that happened in these years in a few words. I had a hard time getting started at first – the South Korean dialect was hard to understand and North Korean refugees aren't treated very well. South Korean capitalism is tough to get used to. It was hard to find my place here, where everything depends on who you know and who you went to school with. When I was angry or frustrated, when I suddenly missed Pyongyang, I always thought of you. If you'd made North Korea into a place worth living in, I'd never have come here. But I didn't want to be sent to one of your prison camps.

Many people here hate you. Watching them, I think of you as a shy boy with fluffy hair, all nervous and shaking in front of the examination table. When did you change so much?

All of North Korea is a prison camp, isn't it? There's no freedom there, only the freedom to trust and obey you and your father. In all North Korea there is only one person who was born free and enjoys the rights due to a human being – you.

I, who left North Korea, pray for you, who made it impossible for me to return to my family. I pray for you because I am your teacher who still remembers you stammering out your Russian test. I pray for North Korea to be opened. I pray that you will repent.

Chairman Kim, it was not easy for me to pray for you – how could it be? I lost my beloved family because of you. When I came to Seoul, I tried to hide my identity, but I heard that you tracked down my relatives and executed them as counterrevolutionaries. If you think you can stop people fleeing your country in this way, you are greatly mistaken.

Chairman Kim, when I would think of my family, I used to hate you so much it almost killed me. The wife who shared my whole life, the sons and daughters we raised together, our daughter-in-law, our beautiful

Photograph courtesy of Kim Hyun-sik

grandchildren – I can't forgive myself for the role I played in their deaths. I've thought of killing myself many times, and spent day after day longing to die.

But I don't want to talk about my grievances against you. I am already more than seventy years old, and I feel my strength failing every day. Before I get too much older, I would like to meet you again. I don't hate you anymore. Even though you killed my family, I have forgiven you.

I am alive, and I will give my remaining strength so that one day God's gospel will be heard in the land where my family sweated, so that one day it will be a land of education that is the envy of the world, and a land of faith that is an example to the world.

Your teacher from the old days,
Kim Hyun-sik

Reconciliations

While in Seoul, I lectured on the Korean War at the National Intelligence Institute to an audience of reserve officers, many of whom had fought in the war. I told how I had been badly wounded by shrapnel from a mortar round. A man in the audience raised his hand and asked,

"Do you remember when and where you were wounded?"

"Of course, how could I forget? The battle in the highlands at Yongan, North Hamgyong, in December 1950."

"Ah . . . I'm very sorry. I was an officer in that battle, and I commanded the mortars."

He bowed his head and apologized respectfully. Suddenly full of rage, I came down from the podium and grabbed him by the shoulders and yelled at him.

"You're doing very well, aren't you, after making me this way! Look at my head! Look at this wound – I lived for twenty-five years with shrapnel in my head. Do you have any idea how much it hurts all the time?"

The anger and sadness that I had pushed down for decades erupted. I kept shouting at him, out of my mind with anger.

"I'm sorry, I'm sorry." He took off his belt and handed it to me. "I was given this belt in recognition of my service when I was discharged from the army. It may not comfort you, but since I cannot give you my heart, I give you my belt instead. Please, take it."

He stood in front of me, his head bowed, pleading for my forgiveness. I took the belt in my hands and forgave him. I still have the belt, and whenever I wear it, I think of his warmth and humility.

I had another surprising experience, this time in America.

In summer 2001, I was sightseeing in Washington, DC, when we came to a tidy neighborhood of one-story houses. All the houses looked exactly the same, not like a regular neighborhood. "These houses were built by the government for widows of American soldiers killed in the Korean War," my guide told me. "Shall we get out?" I followed him.

Many Americans died in the war. They weren't used to the harsh climate. Many died from shells, froze to death in the cold, or starved when supply lines were broken.

After we'd walked a bit, we met an elderly woman sitting on a bench with a boy who looked to be her grandson. She asked me if I was Japanese. I told her I was Korean, and she seized my hand.

"You're from the country where my husband is buried. They couldn't find his body. I just got a letter from the government. But I know he is sleeping somewhere in Korea."

As I watched her eyes fill with tears, I thought back to the winter of 1950 in North Hamgyong when our troops held the high ground in Eoryongchon under constant mortar fire. Every time a mortar landed, our men

Photograph from Clay Gilliland / Wikimedia Commons (public domain)

The demilitarized zone separating North and South Korea

would fall dying. When the attack stopped, there were only three or four men left alive from our platoon of fifty. The enemy moved up toward our position, thinking that we were all dead. When they were only thirty or forty meters away, the sergeant shouted, "Prepare grenades. Arm. Throw!"

The grenades burst deafeningly and the enemy soldiers began to run. The sergeant and the others chased them, throwing more grenades. I couldn't move. Right in front of me, an American soldier was rolling on the ground, his body blown in half. Blood was spurting everywhere.

"Grandmother, forgive me. I was a North Korean soldier. I threw grenades at your husband and many other Americans. Please forgive me."

I bowed my head in front of her. But she wasn't angry at me. She touched the old wounds in my head and arm. "How much did those hurt? You must have been hit by our guns too. I'm also sorry."

She took my hand and prayed. As she prayed, my heart became quiet. I felt that the wounds in my soul from shooting at enemy soldiers, from being brought to the edge of death by their shells, were washed away by her prayer.

I felt God speaking to me through these two seemingly coincidental events. He wanted to change me, to take away memories stained with anger and despair, and to open a new world through forgiveness and reconciliation.

My former student Kim Jong-il died in 2011 – so far as I know, without having repented. Yet I still long for Korea's reunification. It will happen only when we forgive one another and embrace one another in love.

We need the same love that God showed to me through the widow of an American soldier. It's not just a matter of joining together two pieces of land that have been separated. We must respect and accept each other, like two rivers that flow into one another. Isn't that the only true reunification? Isn't that what God wants? ⤳

Translated from Korean by Sung Hoon Park and Raymond Mommsen.

Twilight

Victor says, *I love this time of day.*
This is when I say, Never want to die,
want to be here forever.
O maybe it will be possible, in the shaggy heads of trees
that barely felt us walking beneath them.
Maybe the corners we turned so often
the broken pavements
cracks & signatures
Daniel Lozano 1962
continue to hold us all –
days we walked through thoughtlessly
forgetting to turn our heads
to the vine finally making it over the fence
dangling blossom
orange cup of joy
ephemeral as we were
here
imagining our deep root

NAOMI SHIHAB NYE

Above, Jon Redmond, *Faded Rose Diptych,* 2015

A "child-friendly space" in Kara Tepe refugee camp, Lesbos, Greece. The author is in a red T-shirt, center.

Snapshots from Lesbos

Three Weeks with Children in the Refugee Camps

SHEERA HINKEY

ON SEPTEMBER 22, 2015, I arrived in Lesbos, the Greek island off the Turkish mainland where migrants from Syria, Iraq, and Afghanistan continue to arrive in inflatable dinghies, often four to nine thousand daily. For the next three weeks, I stayed in Kara Tepe and Moria, the two refugee camps, as a volunteer for Save the Children, the international relief organization. Together with a team of twelve others, my job was to set up a

"child-friendly space" in each of the camps – a place where children who had survived crossing the Aegean Sea could play.

During the first days, we'd simply choose a flat spot where no one was sleeping, pick up the empty water bottles and trash, and spread a tarp over the gravel, using rugs and a few scavenged boards to create a playing surface. (Eventually we built a shade structure.) Instantly the kids would arrive, sometimes as

A family rests on a Lesbos beach shortly after arriving on a dinghy from the Turkish coast.

Photographs, *left*, Laura Maendel and, *right*, AP Photo / Santi Palacios

many as forty. I painted butterflies on faces, played soccer, drew hundreds of Crayola pictures, got covered in glitter glue, helped engineer elaborate block towers, and every once in a while looked up to observe the camp around me. What follows are mere snapshots of what I saw – any attempt to draw tidy conclusions would be as inadequate as the makeshift haven we sought to provide. ■

WE SOON LEARNED that many of the Syrian children playing on the tarp had experienced trauma from the war; several had scars we didn't ask about. Often it seemed that every kid under five had wet his pants.

When at play, though, the children laughed and yelled loudly, throwing gravel at each other and arguing over every goal in the soccer game. The younger boys all coveted a toy John Deere tractor that one of the volunteers had brought with him, a gift from a boy in England; as long as the battery held out, it made engine noises and had lights that flashed. Then one morning the tractor disappeared. Nothing surprising there, I thought. But as I packed up the toys into suitcases at the end of the day, a four-year-old ran up to me, tractor in hand. I praised him up and down, in English. He just grinned and ran away. ■

Sheera Hinkey, a web developer, is a member of the Bruderhof and lives in upstate New York.

Two Afghan boys pose minutes after landing.

WE RARELY SAW a child for more than a couple of days, as their families were eager to continue their trek, most often toward Germany. Yet some children stand out in my memory, especially Remye (not her real name). She whirled into our space, a grubby, energetic girl with a wild head of curls that blew everywhere in the dusty wind. After drawing a stack of pictures, she tirelessly used the small slide for hours, then came up to me to get a *farasha* (butterfly) painted on her cheek. That done, she decided to paint my face too. Soon I was being mobbed by five little girls armed with orange paint and glitter. When I looked up, Remye had disappeared.

When later that day a neat little girl in a frilly pink dress and pony tail came up to hug me goodbye, it took me an awkward moment before I realized it was Remye. Her mother had dressed her up for the evening ferry ride to Athens – a brave attempt to be normal in Kara Tepe, even though it meant crouching under a water spigot in your underwear while people queued up behind you. ∎

Moria is the worse of the two camps, a former detention center that lacked anywhere near enough toilets and showers; the ground was strewn with trash and feces. The lines of new arrivals waiting to be registered often stretched hundreds of yards; many families waited twenty-four hours or more in line. Under the Mediterranean sun, people put cardboard or jackets over their heads, but one day the heat was so intense that they lined up their knapsacks – often their only possessions – and waited in the shade.

Steve, a fellow volunteer, would play soccer with the children while their parents waited in line. He told me he often felt stupid kicking a ball among rows of half-sleeping men. But then one of them who spoke English struck up a conversation. The man had finally left Syria, he told Steve, after witnessing a beheading. ■

Starting around four in the afternoon, we distributed portions of rice, lentils, and pita bread – often the migrants' only meal of the day. Women and children queued up in one line and the men in the other, which was often twice as long. We could give out only one serving per person, despite the entreaties of the men, who almost always asked for extra portions, holding up several fingers and claiming "family four" or "children" or "brother."

The first time I helped out, I got flustered and dropped a portion, spilling gooey lentils and rice over my shoes and the feet of the man I was serving. The hundreds of men behind him were pushing him past me, but he just managed to take another dish from my hands before he was out of reach. ■

The Welcome Box Campaign

MATT BIRD

Welcome Boxes

Water cannons and tear gas, razor wire, capsized dinghies. These were the images accompanying Europe's headlines throughout the summer. And then newspaper front pages carried the picture of a toddler face down on a beach in Turkey with waves lapping over his limp body.

How could ordinary people far away from the refugee crisis respond rather than simply feel helpless? For a church in Derby, England, the answer has been "welcome boxes." Inspired by the tradition of giving "Christmas boxes" to those in need, they fill boxes with small gifts and deliver them to newly arrived refugees and migrants living in their city. "You can visit someone in their home with a small gift and be the first person they've ever met in the UK," team leader Karina Martin explains.

Along with the initial box of gifts, trained volunteers take a copy of the city's *Welcome to Derby* book. Later, they make follow-up visits to help the family settle in and to connect with local services such as healthcare and schools.

In the last decade, volunteers have delivered welcome boxes to hundreds of families. Recently one box made its way to a mother who had fled Iraq with her children after rebel groups had captured her husband. Her welcome-box friend helped her get back in touch with him. Later she wrote to the church: "I was alone in this country where I have no brother or sister or husband. But when I met you everything changed – you became my brothers and sisters. I thank God that I met you." She is now waiting to be reunited with her husband, who is trying to make the difficult journey across Europe. In the meantime, she has renewed hope, and a friend to stand with her.

Matt Bird is the founder of Cinnamon Network.
www.cinnamonnetwork.co.uk

A newly arrived family in Moria camp

The registration line in Moria on a blistering day. The wait in line can last twenty-four hours or longer.

A five-month-old baby in Kara Tepe; his family had no money for formula.

TIRED after another hot day on the childcare tarp, I was standing with Heather, another volunteer, near the entrance gate to Kara Tepe. "*Kalispéra!* Good evening!" a Greek man hailed us. "Somebody please help Grandma, please." I looked up and saw an elderly woman making her way up the hill, tottering and crying. Through her tears, she tried to tell us something, gesturing and talking at the same time. Eventually we caught the gist. Her husband – or was it her whole family? – had drowned that day in the crossing to Lesbos. Finally we got her to a chair and helped her sit down. When she pulled off her salty wet shoes, her feet were covered in blisters. ∎

ONE DAY a family with six children put down their bags near our playing area in Kara Tepe. The parents went to stand in line for registration, but the children were so tired from their journey that they just slept, never coming over to play. Since their parents hadn't yet had time to locate a tent, they were lying on cardboard. Some hours after they arrived, I glanced over and saw that the littlest boy – he was about two – had rolled off. His face was in the dirt, and when he snuggled in his sleep, he rubbed his cheeks in the grime. I had no clean blanket with me to put under him. ➤

To support Save the Children's work with refugees and migrants, visit www.savethechildren.org.

The Courage to Forgive

An Interview with Hashim Garrett and Charles Williams

A retired police chief and an ex–gang member have teamed up to address dozens of school assemblies in New York and New Jersey. Their message to young people: forgive. *Plough* asked them to reflect on their unlikely friendship – one all the more striking in a year when police shootings and #BlackLivesMatter continue to make headlines.

Plough: How come a former cop and a former gang member are on speaking terms?

Charles Williams: Clearly we used to be enemies on different ends of the gun, even if we didn't know each other. As a young officer with the New York City Housing Authority police department in the 1980s, I was assigned to patrol in the South Bronx just when the crack epidemic hit. My job was to restore or keep peace, while Hashim, with all due respect, was out to cause havoc and chaos. Had we crossed paths back then, we both would have pulled our guns. And if one of us had made the wrong move, there's a good chance we could have killed each other.

Even as I say that now, I get emotional because the man sitting next to me is my brother, my best friend. How did we get here?

Hashim and I are very different, but we have at least two things in common: we're both human beings, and we've both experienced the power of forgiveness.

Hashim, what's the story from your side?

Hashim Garrett: I grew up in Brooklyn. After my parents separated, I lived with my mother and her boyfriend, who had a drinking problem. While under the influence, he would become abusive and would bang on the metal door of our home. Hearing him, I would lie on the floor of my room crying and praying: "Dear God, please make him stop, in Jesus Christ's name" – even though I was born Muslim.

I was bullied at school, so when I was thirteen I decided to befriend my bullies and joined their gang. Sometimes I would shoot people for money, sometimes just for the thrill. At age fifteen, I found a new group of friends – they were big guys, age eighteen to twenty-one. In that gang, the dirty work was reserved for me, since if we were caught, I as a juvenile would be eligible for a reduced sentence. After a while I realized I was being used and began to object when asked to do things. Ultimately, they decided that they would get rid of me.

On May 7, 1990, my so-called friends knocked on my door and asked me to come outside. I should have known something was wrong, because one of them said, "Yo, when you come out, don't bring the guns."

We go up to the corner and we're talking, the six of us. My friends went across the street to the store – everything seemed normal. Then a kid whom I don't know passes me, and I hear my friend shout: "Look out, run!" I take off. I peep over my shoulder and that kid is standing a few feet behind me with a submachine gun.

I'm running and thinking to myself, "Why are my pants making this funny movement?" All of a sudden, something hard hits my back. As I lie there, I'm thinking, "Just close your eyes and put your head down, because if you move, he's going to walk up and kill you." After a few seconds, he runs off. All of my friends are gone. Why can't I move, why can't I feel my legs?

It was half an hour before the ambulance took me, and I'm bleeding out of twelve holes: six bullets went in, and six bullets exited. I remember looking up at the sky: "God, please don't let me die."

I was in hospital for a month and a half. The doctors told me I would never walk again. (To this day I am paralyzed from the waist down.) I cried like a baby, I was angry, and all I could think about was killing the kid who shot me.

Eventually the police caught him and showed me his picture. "All you got to do is sign here, and he's going to go to jail." I'm from Brooklyn, and we don't snitch. I said, "I don't know what you're talking about." So they let him go, although the detectives were angry since they knew that I was lying. After the shooter was released back onto the streets of Brooklyn, he shot somebody else I knew.

While lying in the rehabilitation facility, I did a lot of soul-searching. One day my mother handed me a Bible. She told me that she didn't have any answers to make me feel better, but maybe this book would help. Reading the Bible made me realize that I didn't need to walk in order to be healed. I needed God's mercy and his spiritual healing. I felt like I didn't deserve to walk again. I was evil, and I must pay for my terrible deeds. My prayer was that God would have mercy on me on the Day of Judgment.

In a way, the day I was shot was the best day of my life, because it was the day I began to be freed from anger and hate. My father was so angry about my injury that he asked me if I

Interview by Peter Mommsen on October 19, 2015. Watch the video at plough.com/breakingthecycle.

Photograph courtesy of John Noltner www.apeaceofmymind.net

wanted him to kill the shooter. I told him no. I needed God to forgive me. I realized that it was my fault that this happened to me. I also realized that I was very fortunate to be alive, so I didn't want to go back to making poor decisions.

In the early 2000s, friends encouraged me to start speaking to teenagers about gangs. Through this work, in 2006 I was invited to join the Breaking the Cycle anti-violence program founded by Bruderhof pastor Johann Christoph Arnold and New York police detective Steven McDonald, who in 1986 was also shot and paralyzed, but from the neck down – he needs a respirator to breathe.

Dozens of times, I watched Detective McDonald and Pastor Arnold talk to students about forgiveness, and that built up my courage to talk about forgiveness too. It was amazing to me how week after week, Pastor Arnold would get up in front of hundreds of high school students and tell them how forgiveness can help them – despite the fifty-year age gap. Until then, I had always thought forgiveness was a sign of weakness and that kids wouldn't respect that message. But coming from him, they embraced it and appreciated it.

Would you say that you had forgiven the person who shot you?

Hashim: Yes, although I never spoke to the kid and told him I forgave him. Being around Pastor Arnold gave me a clearer vision of what forgiveness means and what role it needs to play in my life. I had to forgive the shooter and forgive my parents. And I had to forgive myself – that's the hardest.

I am blessed to have a beautiful wife and two beautiful children. Being a spouse with a disability is a test. I can't play in the ocean with my children, I can't teach them how to ride a bicycle. However, my children do know

Hashim Garrett with his wife Maya and their children

Photograph courtesy of Hashim Garrett

that their father loves them very much. When I am home, I play with them, hug them, bathe them, feed them, read with them, and most importantly, we pray together.

With my wife Maya – I am unable to dance with her. For her, having a husband with a disability is not easy. She once wrote this about our marriage:

> Ninety-five percent is blissful: our relationship is normal, wonderful – what you would expect from any healthy marriage. Then there is the other 5 percent, when I'm reminded of my husband's injury. There are moments when I feel completely overwhelmed by this, and the 5 percent feels insurmountable. But I remind myself to keep things in perspective, that I too have scars, emotional ones, yet my husband loves me.
>
> I pray and ask God for renewed strength, and God always answers. I married Hashim for four reasons: I love him, he fears God, I believe in the purpose that God has for his life, and Hashim has ambition. How ironic that I would be a stay-at-home mother to our children, and Hashim, with a spinal cord injury, would be the sole provider. Hashim wants to be used by God; I feel privileged to witness this every day.

As a Muslim, my faith in the Creator helps me realize that what I'm doing is bigger than me. My goal is to spread a message of reconciliation. Since the Creator has all things in his hands, I don't need to worry whether or not I see the fruit of my labor. My job is to sow the seeds.

Chief Williams, how did your story intersect with Hashim's?

Charles: I also am one of the people whose lives have been changed by hearing Pastor Arnold and Steven McDonald. In 2002, I attended one of their presentations on forgiveness as chief of police of Cornwall-on-Hudson, New York. On

Charles Williams

the one hand, I was mesmerized. "Wow, what a great message – teaching kids how to deal with conflict in a nonviolent manner." On the other hand, I felt I could never forgive someone who shot me. It seemed impossible, too heroic.

Afterward, as I was describing the event to a colleague, it suddenly struck me that the reason I couldn't imagine how Steven McDonald forgave the shooter was because I myself had someone I needed to forgive, but couldn't: my mother.

Throughout my childhood, my mother was a raging alcoholic. As a six-year-old, I would watch her throwing furniture, fighting off my father, and screaming. One day in elementary school, I came home to find her passed out in a chair. Next morning she was still there, surrounded by burns in the carpet from her cigarette – we could have died in a fire during the night.

Growing up, I felt that my mother loved alcohol more than she loved me. She didn't care what I looked like, what I smelled like, if my clothes were clean, or if my homework was done. I *hated* that woman.

I hated her as a kid, I hated her in high school, I hated her when I was dating, I hated her in college, and I hated her while at the police academy. I thought nobody could tell. But it had effects. I was not a good husband; I separated from my wife. I could have been a better father, and I could have been a better cop.

But through hearing Detective McDonald and Pastor Arnold, my life changed. I decided to forgive my mother. I drove down to Long Island, back to my hometown, and called my mother when I was about fifteen minutes away. I got her answering machine. I thought, "Perfect – now I have an excuse not to do this." I almost turned around. But something deep inside told me, "No – now is the time." So I left her a message, and she called back.

I went into the house and sat down opposite her. It wasn't easy. And yet something happened. This person in front of me – this person who had made my childhood a nightmare, who in my mind's eye was a crazed monster with a wild look in her eyes – instantaneously changed into a frail, sickly, old woman on oxygen, dying of emphysema. She became the mother I had never had.

She said, "I want to make it right." I told her, "Mom, I forgive you. You don't have to make anything right."

Now, it wasn't like a movie. My mother never apologized, and we didn't hug. It just ended. I felt fifty years of hate and anger dropping off of me.

As a result of these experiences, both of you joined the Breaking the Cycle team, sharing your stories with thousands of young people. How do they react?

Charles: After an assembly we're surrounded by kids who want to tell us their stories – what's going on with them at home or in school. We're strangers, of course. But the reason they want to talk is that in our presentation we open up, we show that we're vulnerable. A young girl told us she had walked down the corridor and heard us speaking – she wasn't supposed to be there. But she was intrigued and drawn in. After the assembly she came down to Hashim and me and said, "You guys saved my life. I was going to kill myself today."

"Forgiveness in Charleston isn't absolution for four hundred years of racial violence in America," ran one recent headline, referring to victims' families who forgave the killer in the Emanuel church shooting. Your response?

Hashim: It makes sense to me when people go, "If someone hurts my family, then I will retaliate. If I forgive them, how will they feel my pain?" It seems like letting them off the hook. One reason forgiveness is criticized, I think, is that it takes courage to forgive. It doesn't take courage to be violent; cowards can strike back. But to remain nonviolent you must be brave.

Charles: Those who criticize forgiveness don't understand that it doesn't mean condoning the act. For me, it simply meant letting go of the pain, anger, distrust, and betrayal of the past, all of which was negatively affecting my present. Through forgiving, I was leaving the past where it belonged. And forgiveness really

Photograph courtesy of Charles Williams

has nothing to do with justice. People easily confuse the two, thinking that if they forgive the perpetrator, he won't be held accountable. But justice is up to the courts of law, and ultimately, justice is up to God. That has nothing to do with me, nor does it have anything to do with forgiveness.

But how does forgiveness apply to justice in a broader sense – such as the issue of police misconduct? In recent months, there's been extensive coverage of police killings of people such as Eric Garner, Michael Brown, Walter Scott, and Freddie Gray.

Hashim: I can't pretend that there aren't problems in our society that need to be addressed, laws that need to be changed, and policies that need to be reformed and improved. But I also think it is important to realize that we can't be so judgmental. For me, it's important to share this message with my community. We can't judge all police officers based on the ones that we see on the news making poor decisions. That is one thing I have learned from working with Chief Williams and Detective Steven McDonald. It's difficult for me now to look at the news and go, "All cops are bad because that one cop did something bad." I know good police officers.

Chief Williams, how is forgiveness relevant to the law enforcement profession?

Charles: Looking back, the issue that my brothers and sisters in law enforcement face is not taking things personally – because if someone's trying to hurt you, how do you *not* take it personally? Here's a common mistake: if I had been called to a really bad domestic dispute, or if someone had physically fought me, and if I didn't let the anger and stress go, then I would carry it into my next vehicle traffic stop. The next interaction could turn very negative.

Johann Christoph Arnold founded Breaking the Cycle with Steven McDonald, a New York City police officer, in 1999.

Just imagine carrying that anger and stress for fifteen years straight as a police officer.

The answer is to forgive after every call. When you talk to individual officers, they get it, though I don't know how much they can put into practice because of the culture: many police-related organizations don't want anything to do with forgiveness because they think it's weak. But that's not true; forgiveness is about not letting a bad experience cause you to make a potentially deadly error in your next interaction.

When the two of you speak together in schools, what do the students ask you?

Hashim: I don't think I've ever had a kid come up to me and say, "I don't like police officers." In fact, they rarely mention law enforcement as a problem. Their biggest problems are being bullied, or being afraid to walk home because of gangs. Or, "I don't think my mom and dad love me." I find that no matter what school district we go into, self-hate is universal – whether in the form of cutting, or suicide, or gang violence. You can't love yourself if you're going to go out and kill; you can't love yourself if you sit in your bathroom cutting your wrist.

What changes in teenagers' concerns have you noticed during nine years of doing this work?

Hashim: Social media, of course, plays an increasing role. So many kids seem to feel

The
Breaking
the Cycle
team in
Ramsey,
New Jersey,
2014

alone, even when sitting in a room with a hundred kids. Ultimately, the solution to online bullying remains the same. If someone is trolling you, the answer is still forgiveness. Suicide is not the answer. Have the courage to forgive them.

After we're done speaking, many kids come up and say, "Can I shake your hand?" It strikes me that they want to feel a real connection.

Charles: In the same way, at the end of every event we offer students copies of Pastor Arnold's book *Why Forgive?*, which includes Hashim's and my story. Usually they want us to sign the books for that physical connection: "Yeah, that's the guy I saw. There's his handwriting."

Hashim: We've had parents contact us after one of our events saying, "I don't know what you said, but my kid came home and talked to me today. He didn't just say, 'Oh, school was fine,' and go in his room and close the door. He sat down, showed me Arnold's book, and told me about this assembly. Thank you." When I hear about kids reconnecting with their parents, I know we've made progress.

I remember being that fifteen-year-old kid lying in the hospital who didn't want to live anymore, who wanted to hurt those who had hurt him. That helps me not to be judgmental. You can judge the act, but not the person. I don't know what was going on in Adam Lanza's life when he entered the school in Newtown, Connecticut, with his guns. But what if someone could have spoken to him earlier about forgiveness, in a way he could connect to? Maybe that would have made a difference. ➤

Read fifty stories of forgiveness, including Charles Williams's and Hashim Garrett's, in Johann Christoph Arnold's book Why Forgive? *(Plough, 2010). To learn more about Breaking the Cycle, visit* www.breakingthecycle.com.

William Harnett, *Still Life with Ginger Jar*

INSIGHTS *on* MERCY

Fyodor Dostoyevsky Every day and whenever you can, repeat to yourself, "Lord, have mercy on all who appear before you today." For every hour and every moment thousands of men leave life on this earth, and their souls appear before God. And how many of them depart in solitude, unknown, sad, dejected that no one mourns for them or even knows whether they have lived or not? Behold, from the other end of the earth, perhaps, your prayer for their rest will rise up to God, though you knew them not nor they you. How must it feel to a soul standing in dread before the Lord to sense at such an instant that for him too there is one to pray, that there is a fellow creature left on earth to love him too? God will look on you both more graciously, for if you have had pity on him, how much more will he have pity, who is infinitely more loving and merciful than you? And he will forgive him for your sake.

Graham Greene There was a man, a good man, a holy man, and he lived in sin all through his life, because he couldn't bear the idea that any soul could suffer damnation. This man decided that if any soul was going to be damned, he would be damned too. He never took the sacraments, he never married his wife in church. I don't know, my child, but some people think he was – well, a saint. I think he died in what we are told is mortal sin – I'm not sure . . . You can't conceive, my child, nor can I or anyone, the appalling strangeness of the mercy of God.

Julian of Norwich Mercy is a sweet, gracious working in love, mingled with plenteous pity: for mercy works in keeping us, and mercy works turning for us all things to good. Mercy, by love, suffers us to fail in measure and inasmuch as we fail, in so much we fall; and inasmuch as we fall, in so much we die: for it needs must be that we die in so much as we fail of the sight and feeling of God that is our life. Our failing is dreadful, our falling is shameful, and our dying is sorrowful: but in all this the sweet eye of pity and love is lifted never off us, nor does the working of mercy cease.

Eberhard Arnold You must give yourself up totally so as to win back your life made utterly new, with unsuspected abilities and powers. Have the patience and courage to begin anew each day, and trust in God's help; his mercy is new every morning. Then you will understand that life is always a matter of becoming or growing, and that you must always look forward to greater things. Even though you stand in battle with dark powers, the victory will be yours, since in Christ every evil is overcome. ➳

Sources: Fyodor Dostoyevsky, *The Brothers Karamazov,* trans. C. Garnett (Macmillan, 1922), 339. Graham Greene, *Brighton Rock* (Penguin, 1991), 246 (abridged). Julian of Norwich, *Revelations of Divine Love,* ed. G. Warrack (Methuen and Co., 1901), 101. Eberhard Arnold, June 10, 1921, in Johann Christoph Arnold, *Seeking Peace* (Plough, 1998), 162.

Rembrandt Harmenszoon van Rijn, *Repentant Judas Returning the Pieces of Silver*, 1629

Forgiving the Unforgivable?

On Guilt and Pardon

HANNA-BARBARA GERL-FALKOVITZ

*Are there any limits to forgiveness? In this essay, Gerl-Falkovitz
helps us plumb the depth of that question, showing why
forgiveness is not something to be taken lightly.*

STORIES OF FORGIVENESS, *as the media has discovered, touch us powerfully. Who can forget the forgiveness offered by victims' families after the recent church shooting in Charleston, South Carolina? Earlier, the families of Coptic Christians martyred by ISIS forgave the killers, as did the families of the Amish schoolgirls murdered in 2006 in Nickel Mines, Pennsylvania.*

Yet as the divided reactions to these cases show, for many forgiveness is suspect, even offensive. It seems too simple, too easy, a denial of the horror of the crime. At best, it's dismissed as a weak concession to the need for closure; at worst, it's condemned as an insult to the dead.

Seldom has the protest against cheap "forgiving and forgetting" been raised more eloquently than by Vladimir Jankélévitch (1903–1985), who as a Jew had joined the French Resistance to the Nazis. Gerl-Falkovitz takes his response to the Holocaust as her starting point.

—The Editors

"SHOULD WE PARDON THEM?" That was the question posed by the French philosopher Vladimir Jankélévitch in a 1971 essay of that title about Nazi war crimes.[1] Jankélévitch passionately opposed a statute of limitations for these atrocities.[2] He argued that crimes against humanity – those committed in Auschwitz, for example – are dehumanizing in the most basic sense: they attack the very essence of what it is to be human. Crimes like these, he wrote, cannot be covered by reconciliation:

> It was the very being of humanity, *esse,* that racial genocide attempted to annihilate in the suffering flesh of these millions of martyrs. . . . When an act denies the essence of a human being as a human being, the statutory limitations that urge absolution in the name of morality actually themselves contradict morality.[3]

Forgiveness, according to Jankélévitch, died in the concentration camps. (His essay had a powerful effect: as a result of it, in France there was no statute of limitations for Nazi collaborators under the Vichy regime.)

Jankélévitch then went on to ask what is required for reconciliation to be possible. Since both victims and perpetrators are dead, to whom could forgiveness be directed? Can the state "forgive"? Doubtless it can do so in the sense of granting a pardon and waiving punishment, but not in the sense of actually erasing guilt. Who then could grant such all-encompassing forgiveness?

Jankélévitch assumes that only a personal forgiveness is possible – a face-to-face forgiveness between torturers and victims, in a private encounter without any third parties. But this requires that the victim is still alive – if not, then the door to forgiveness has slammed shut.

The author is professor emeritus of philosophy at Dresden University and head of EUPHRat (European Institute for Philosophy and Religion) at Hochschule Heiligenkreuz. Her book on forgiveness is titled Verzeihung des Unverzeihlichen? Ausflüge in Landschaften der Schuld und der Vergebung *(2013).*

In that case, the torturer's remorse achieves nothing; it is inadequate and comes too late. Remorse is decoupled from forgiveness; the two are separated by an unbridgeable gap in time.

In Jankélévitch's view, later generations may not presume to offer forgiveness – something they are not entitled to do in any case, in view of the sheer monstrosity of the guilt. When politics engages in the rituals of official apology, it is overstepping its proper boundaries in pursuit of a strategic benefit: apology becomes a semi-sacred event for the public. The rhetoric bandied over the mass graves is impure, even if it is the victims' grandchildren who are speaking:

Thanks to indifference, moral amnesia, and general superficiality, pardoning today is a fait accompli. Everything is already long forgiven and forgotten.[4]

Nevertheless, Jankélévitch argues, the guilt still exists, since the agony of the victims "will remain until the end of days." No handshakes, no yearning for social harmony on the part of later generations, can salvage what is unforgivable.

Now for a contrasting picture: Eva Mozes Kor and her twin sister, born to a Jewish family, were used for medical experiments on humans by the SS doctor Josef Mengele.[5] As she remembers it, she was defined by her status as victim. Half a century later, she met with

EVA MOZES KOR

Forgiving Dr. Mengele

At the age of ten, Eva Mozes Kor and her twin sister Miriam were transported to Auschwitz. There Dr. Josef Mengele used the two girls along with other twins for medical experiments. Mozes Kor, who speaks internationally, went on to found the CANDLES Holocaust Museum in Terre Haute, Indiana.

Eva Mozes Kor, *far right,* and other young survivors of Auschwitz in January 1945

ON JANUARY 27, 1945, four days before my eleventh birthday, Auschwitz was liberated by the Soviet army. I returned to my village in

Romania to find that no one from my family other than Miriam had survived.

Forty years passed before I spoke to Miriam about our experiences in Auschwitz. She died in 1993 from the long-term effects of Mengele's experiments. That year I was invited to lecture to some doctors in Boston and was asked if I could bring a Nazi doctor with me. I thought it was a mad request until I remembered that I'd once been in a documentary which had also featured a Dr. Hans Münch from Auschwitz, who had known Mengele. I contacted him in Germany and he agreed to meet with me for a videotaped interview. On my way to meet this Nazi doctor, I was so scared, but when I arrived at his home he treated me with the utmost respect. I asked him if he'd seen the gas chambers. He said this was a nightmare he dealt with every day of his life. I was surprised that Nazis had nightmares too and asked him if he would come with me to Auschwitz to sign a document at the ruins of the gas chambers. He agreed.

another SS doctor, Hans Münch, who asked her for forgiveness. It was then that she recognized in his appeal a way to leave behind the harm inflicted on her. The "helpless little Mengele guinea pig," in her words, possessed something she hadn't been aware of: the power to forgive. By means of this power, which she had not previously suspected and which now overwhelmed her, she freed herself from the shadow of a lifelong status as a victim. She pronounced forgiveness and found freedom – including freedom in the face of accusations that she had betrayed her dead sister. Mozes Kor did not see it that way; for her, forgiveness was a way to honor the dead – perhaps the only appropriate way. It was a way that transcended all the requirements of a just punishment. The logic of retribution paled in light of her experience that forgiveness offers a way of liberation for both perpetrators and victims.

The Reappearance of Guilt

Jankélévitch's words about an essential, unredeemable guilt brought a bleak and long-forgotten tone back into the business of "processing the past." Ever since Nietzsche and Freud, it had become usual to classify guilt in terms of unresolved "guilt feelings," which could be treated by therapy. Wasn't the sense of being guilty, produced by cultural conditioning, the sum total of what guilt was?

In my desperate effort to find a meaningful thank-you gift for Dr. Münch, I searched the stores, and my heart, for many months. Then the idea of a forgiveness letter came to my mind. I knew it would be a meaningful gift for Dr. Münch, but even more important, it became a gift to myself. I realized I was not a hopeless, powerless victim. When I asked a friend to check my spelling, she challenged me to forgive Mengele too. At first I was adamant that I could never do that. But with time, I realized that now it was I who had the power: the power to forgive. It was my right to use it. No one could take it away.

On January 27, 1995, at the fiftieth anniversary of the liberation of Auschwitz, I stood by the ruins of the gas chambers with my children, next to Dr. Münch and his children and grandchild. Dr. Münch signed his document about the operation of the gas chambers while I read my document of forgiveness and signed it. As I did that, I felt a burden of pain lifted from me. I was no longer in the grip of hate; I was finally free.

The day I forgave the Nazis, I also privately forgave my parents, whom I had hated all my life for not having saved me from Auschwitz. Children expect their parents to protect them; mine couldn't. And then I forgave myself for hating my parents.

I believe with every fiber of my being that every human being has the right to live without the pain of the past. For most people there is a big obstacle to forgiveness because society expects revenge. We need to honor and remember our victims, but I always wonder if my dead loved ones would want me to live with pain and anger until the end of my life. Some survivors do not want to let go of the pain. They call me a traitor and accuse me of speaking in their name. I have never done that. Forgiveness is as personal as chemotherapy – I do it for myself.

To learn more about Eva Mozes Kor's work, visit www.candlesholocaustmuseum.org.

The end of the twentieth century, however, brought increasing attention to the history of crimes committed in the name of what Ernst Bloch called "the humane human being"

(*der menschliche Mensch*). Ideologies of various hues, whether communist, fascist, or liberal-capitalist, had denied the humanity of millions because of their race or class, and had done so not in the name of any god but rather in the name of the advance of "humanization."

This guilt has stacked up into an unbearably heavy inheritance for today's generations. And shall it remain into all eternity? Auschwitz is one symbol of this guilt, and there are others too: the Gulag Archipelago, Pol Pot, the Chinese Cultural Revolution, Rwanda . . . Meanwhile at this very moment, ISIS, al-Qaeda, and Boko Haram are carrying out killings in the Middle East and Nigeria in the name of an Islamist god. Horrors that had seemed to be a thing of the past are now back with a vengeance. Guilt, shorn of any disguise, has reentered the language of politics, faith, and philosophy.

The turn of the millennium was accompanied by a rash of apologies for guilt: the Boers apologized to the Khoikhoi, European Australians to the Aborigines, US politicians to the Native Americans. Before that, there were German gestures of penitence such as Chancellor Willy Brandt's 1970 visit to the Warsaw Ghetto, when he fell on his knees to commemorate the dead. Yet in these apologies, the addressee has rarely been named clearly. In a non-religious world, who was the one who might grant forgiveness? The exception to this pattern is telling: in 2000, when Pope John Paul II asked forgiveness for the historic guilt of Christians, he appealed neither to the dead nor to their descendants, but to God.

Jankélévitch specifically rejected the wishful dream that the descendants of the victims could (or should) forgive the descendants of the murderers. Neither group, he argued, is directly involved in the crime, even if they are caught up in its aftermath. But how then can one reach the dead torturers and victims? Time cannot be rolled back. What does forgiveness actually accomplish – if forgiveness is to mean something more than just the restoration of social harmony?

Most basically: Who is it who forgives? What difference does it make to the crime or to the criminal – if any?

Pure Gift: A Prelude to Pure Forgiveness
In order to understand *forgiving,* not least in its biblical depth of meaning, we must first reflect on *giving.* The basis of any economy is exchange – a fair balance of giving and receiving. Exchange represents a pragmatic justice that evens things out. In its drastic form, the concept of exchange is linked to the rule of "an eye for an eye, a tooth for a tooth."

Yet where human beings are balanced against things, where value is balanced against price, and where life itself is balanced against money and commodities, the blurry and debasing nature of exchange shows up clearly. To take a well-known example: "And they took the thirty pieces of silver, the price of the one on whom a price had been set, on whom some of the people of Israel had set a price . . ." (Matt. 27:9). Thirty coins are the "balance" that is exchanged for the Son of Man; when these coins are thrown back into the temple, they can just as easily be used to buy a potter's field. Exchange breaks down when things that are unlike are treated as if they were alike. As this relates to our topic here: can murder ever be "balanced out," or atoned for, or forgiven – even in exchange for remorse?

The opposite of exchange is the "pure gift." Such a gift is supererogatory: it is above and beyond any price, any equivalent value, or any debt owed. Such a gift is gratuitousness itself, it is pure grace. "If anyone wants to sue you and take your coat, give your cloak as well; and if anyone forces you to go one mile, go also the second mile" (Matt. 5:40–41). A pure gift is not given according to the logic of the Roman motto *do ut des* – "I give that you might give to me" – but rather in another sense: "I give because I have received." Exact repayment is transformed into an attitude of free and unselfish giving-on to others.

The clearest example of this is love. Love cannot be balanced out through justice; love exists only when it is *not* owed, when it is freely offered. This pure gift is the heart of creation, and for Christians, it's more: it is the heart of the still greater redemption to come.

Pure Forgiveness: A Bridge to the Divine

Taking stock of the horrors of the twentieth century, Jacques Derrida (1930–2004) proposed a heightened form of "pure *giving*": he called it "pure *forgiving*." (Derrida plays on the French terms *don pur*, "pure gift," and *pardon pur*, "pure forgiveness.") He did this expressly to oppose Jankélévitch's bitter essay "Should We Pardon Them?," arguing against putting conditions on forgiveness and thus turning it into a commodity to be exchanged.

Derrida speaks instead of the necessity for "pure absolution" from guilt: absolution as unconditional forgiveness, offered without receiving anything in exchange. For-*giving* doesn't depend on balancing guilt with expiation. That's why forgiveness cannot be a provision in criminal law: it must remain outside of any balancing of legal rights. After

all, to pardon a criminal means setting aside the law, and can only ever be done as an exception; but the act of pardoning arises from the transcendent "mystical foundation" of a justice that legal justice cannot catch up with.[6]

Derrida takes aim at Jankélévitch's first thesis – that forgiveness may only be granted (if at all) in a one-on-one encounter of perpetrator and victim. If the possibility of forgiveness really ended with the death of the victim, then the perpetrator's remorse would come too late; the perpetrator would no longer have an active role in the drama. Remorse and forgiveness would then be logically separated: *forgiving* would no longer have a *giver,* indeed forgiveness itself would become mortal. Derrida asks: can forgiveness really be so time-bound, so finite? And even more seriously: is forgiveness then actually something that is "exchanged" for remorse?

Derrida also detects in Jankélévitch's second thesis a concealed logic of exchange, here in negative form: for certain crimes such as crimes against humanity, no adequate compensation could ever be offered. What sort of remorse could ever free a concentration camp commander from his guilt?

Derrida concludes that it must be possible – perhaps it is even necessary? – to break this cycle of guilt and expiation. To that end, he turns to the biblical story of the original sin: the Bible speaks of the great sin of Adam and Eve (Gen. 3), but it speaks  too of Yahweh's a priori forgiveness, granted already before the first sin was committed (see Exod. 6–10). Grace is more than a concept, a speculation, or a wish – grace "already is."[7]

Forgiveness then, according to Derrida, must extend to forgiving the unforgivable:

It is necessary, it seems to me, to begin from the fact that, yes, there is the unforgivable. Is this not, in truth, the only thing to forgive? The only thing that *calls* for forgiveness? If one is only prepared to forgive what appears forgivable, what the church calls "venial sin," then the very idea of forgiveness would disappear. If there is something to forgive, it would be what in religious language is called "mortal sin," the worst, the unforgivable crime or harm. . . . There is only forgiveness, if there is any, where there is the unforgivable. That is to say that forgiveness must announce itself as impossibility itself. It can only be possible in doing the impossible. . . . What would be a forgiveness that forgave only the forgivable?[8]

In other words: absolution is only possible in the sphere of the *absolute,* not in the *relative* sphere of human score-settling. What lies concealed behind this "absolute"?

Derrida's argument accords with the biblical way of thinking: the Abrahamic faiths all recognize the possibility of an unimaginable forgiveness. Indeed, Derrida mentions the

Catholic church, which actually offers such forgiveness. (Although Derrida, as a Jew, does not belong to the church, he is likely thinking of the Catholic practice of confession.) Pure forgiveness, in his view, can only come into being when the confrontation between two people (even if both are dead) is resolved through the presence of Another: a Giver of forgiveness who is not bound by time. The dimension of this Other transcends the realm of human possibilities while drawing them toward the horizon of what is impossible, yet nevertheless imaginable:

Is forgiveness a matter for human beings, something belonging to humankind and within the scope of human capability – or is it reserved to God? . . . Is it divine/otherworldly or this-worldly, consecrated/holy or not? All debates about forgiveness have to do with this boundary and with trespasses of this boundary.[9]

In contrast to rituals of political renewal, then, forgiveness involves something more.

Sending Guilt Back into Nothingness

Can what has been done be undone through forgiveness? Certainly, the mystery of evil cannot be solved by erasing history (2 Thess. 2:7). Augustine's insight is relevant here: according to him, sin serves to build up a false reality (he calls it the "privation of good"). Fundamentally, evil can exercise its power only by using a stolen mask – it works only under the false pretense of being good. The lie consists of inflating evil, as if it *were* something good.

In no way does this deny or diminish the horrible reality of guilt or the irretrievable absence of the victims. Forgiveness means neither undoing the crime nor belittling its horror. Face-to-face with the absolute, something else happens instead: evil is exposed as futile, void, nonsensical, even miserable – and it is then sent back (*remissio*) into the nothingness out of which it emerged. Evil disappears in the nothingness of its usurped power, extinguished in its claim to be "something." What does this mean?

Indulgentiam, absolutionem et remissionem peccatorum nostrorum – so runs the prayer for forgiveness in the Roman Mass, which literally asks for "*clemency* for, *freeing* from, and *sending back* of our sins." *Remissio* refers to an objective process: sending evil back into its nullity, returning the lie back into its non-being. Forgiveness directs our gaze toward the past, but only in order to allow the past to vanish by itself into its own nothingness.

Forgiveness takes away from the past its power to remain present – to remain in the appalling "eternal now" of which Jankélévitch speaks.[10] Forgiveness frees the present and the future from the corpse of what has been.

Forgiveness, then, doesn't remember the past in order to keep it eternally present. Rather, the past is sent back and vanishes, and forgiveness forgets it. This is the sense in which God will, in the words of Psalm 103, "cast our sins behind us" – "as far as the morning is from the evening," to translate Jerome's rendering literally. As the Psalmist declares:

> Bless the Lord . . . who forgives all your iniquity, who heals all your diseases, who redeems your life from the Pit, who crowns you with steadfast love and mercy. . . . He does not deal with us according to our sins, nor repay us according to our iniquities. For as the heavens are high above the earth, so great is his steadfast love toward those who fear him; as far as the east is from the west, so far he removes our transgressions from us. As a father has compassion for his children, so the Lord has compassion for those who fear him.

Augustine remarks: "To the rejected he has promised glory."[11]

Echoing this, the sinner can only say with Kierkegaard: "That you have forgotten and forgiven, I will always keep in remembrance."[12]

Forgiving thus becomes a gift in an augmented sense: it means giving back (*remissio*) what is death-bringing into its own death.

Happy Guilt?

According to Augustine, the most elementary meaning of life is summed up in the phrase *videntem videre* – to see the One who has always seen me. Or in Nicholas of Cusa's words: "Your seeing is your enlivening. . . . Your seeing is your working."[13]

God's gaze and our insatiable looking back to him are something far different than our relationship to anonymous abstractions such as justice or forgiveness. To see, to let ourselves be seen, brings a greater joy than dissolving into a Universal Everything or Universal Nothing. To forgive, then, does not mean sinking back into detachment, but rather it means entering into a new, exhilarating relationship: to another human being, but even more deeply, to the source of life, to God.

Seen this way, forgiveness is grasped not as the neutral cancelation of guilt, but in terms of a Person who is the source of forgiveness. One pebble does not forgive another pebble, nor does the second pebble experience remorse. To repent and to forgive are not mechanical processes. They are acts carried out by persons.

Each year on the night before Easter, the *Exsultet* hymn is sung in churches around the world. This joyous hymn includes the words of Augustine:

> This is the night that with a pillar of fire banished the darkness of sin. This is the night that, even now throughout the world, sets Christian believers apart from worldly vices and from the gloom of sin . . . when Christ broke the prison bars of death and rose victorious from the underworld. Our birth would have been no gain, had we not been redeemed. . . . O truly necessary sin of Adam, destroyed completely by the death of Christ! O happy fault (*felix culpa*) that earned for us so great, so glorious a Redeemer! . . . The sanctifying power of this night dispels wickedness, washes faults away, restores innocence to the fallen, and joy to mourners.[14]

C. S. Lewis once remarked that the apostle Peter, in his later life, would likely have told everyone the story of how he betrayed the Lord – and done so with a radiant face, since on that night he had been drawn into an unimaginable depth of love through a single

glance: "The Lord turned and looked at Peter. . . . And he went out and wept bitterly" (Luke 22:61–62). Only in this light can we grasp the decisive statement: *Guilt is only felt where there is forgiveness.* Normally we think that guilt comes first, then remorse, then forgiveness. This reflects ordinary human experience. But it is not true of God: it is Jesus' glance of forgiveness that prompts the pain of remorse, which in turn brings about an awareness of guilt.

In God's way of redemption, remorse is not made a condition for "pure forgiveness." The "happy fault" not only dissolves this chain of connection, but it also puts the remorseful person's insight into his guilt onto a different basis. The divine goodness that eternally sees every moment in time has already – long before

there was any guilt – opened up a place where guilt *is permitted* to speak itself out and be confessed. Confession is already the first fruit of forgiveness. The glance of love is itself the basis on which evil is repented of. In other words, guilt can only truly be confessed when it comes *face-to-face with forgiveness.*

What is more, when guilt is confessed, it has already begun to disappear. One might say that guilt only becomes evident when it comes within reach of divine forgiveness. Only as our burden is being lifted do we feel its weight.

Divine forgiveness is an unconditional gift that "overtakes" remorse. Remorse isn't what brings on forgiveness, but the opposite: forgiveness draws out remorse – not as a *condition* for finding freedom, but as a *result* of an overwhelming experience. It is in this moment that guilt becomes happy, for it has found its liberator: "Wave upon wave gushes out of you inexhaustible, ever-flowing, billows of water and blood . . . rushing over the deserts of guilt, enriching overabundantly, overflowing every heart that receives it, far surpassing every desire."[15]

Translated from German by Peter Mommsen.

1. Hanna-Barbara Gerl-Falkovitz, *Verzeihung des Unverzeihlichen? Ausflüge in Landschaften der Schuld und der Vergebung* (Text & Dialog, 2013).

2. Vladimir Jankélévitch, "Should We Pardon Them?," trans. Ann Hobart, *Critical Inquiry* 22, no. 3 (1996): 552–572.

3. Ibid., 555–556. (Translation here by Peter Mommsen.)

4. Ibid., 566.

5. Eva Mozes Kor, interview with Harald Welzer, *Frankfurter Rundschau*, June 13, 2003.

6. Jacques Derrida, "Force of Law: The Mystical Foundation of Authority," in *Deconstruction and the Possibility of Justice,* ed. Drucilla Cornell et al. (Routledge, 1992), 3–66.

7. Jacques Derrida, *Pardonner: L'impardonnable et l'imprescriptible* (Galilée, 2005), 70.

8. Jacques Derrida, "On Forgiveness," trans. Michael Hughes, in *On Cosmopolitanism and Forgiveness*

(London & New York: Routledge, 2001), 32–36. See also Derrida, "Das Jahrhundert der Vergebung: Verzeihen ohne Macht – unbedingt und jenseits der Souveränität," interview by Michel Wieviorka, in *Lettre international* 48 (Spring, 2000): 10–18.

9. Derrida, *Pardonner,* 74–75.

10. Vladimir Jankélévitch, "Schuld und Vergebung," in *Sinn und Form: Beiträge zur Literatur* 50, no. 3 (1998): 378.

11. Aurelius Augustinus, *Enarratio in Psalmos,* 110 (109), 1.

12. Søren Kierkegaard, "Love Hides the Multiplicity of Sins," in *Taten der Liebe* (1847), GW 19 (1966), 309ff.

13. Nicholas of Cusa, *De visione Dei* 4,13, 5,18, in *Complete Philosophical and Theological Treatises of Nicholas of Cusa,* trans. Jasper Hopkins (Arthur J. Banning, 2001), 685–687.

14. *The Roman Missal, Third Edition* (ICEL, 2010).

15. Hans Urs von Balthasar, *The Heart of the World,* trans. Erasmo S. Leiva (Ignatius Press, 1979), 153.

Henry Ossawa Tanner, *The Annunciation*, 1898

The God Who Descends

Face to Face with the Incarnation

CHARLES E. MOORE

"All manmade religion stands in opposition to the gospel. It is an ascent toward the eternal, perfect God. Up, up – that is its call. God is high above, we are down below; and now we shall soar by means of our moral, spiritual, and religious endeavors out of the earthly, human depths into the divine heights." —Emil Brunner

"DIVINE HEIGHTS" – yes, that's where most of us want to be: that sphere of bliss where all is well and pure and good and holy, where all that burdens and weighs us down is lifted. Isn't this what religion and spirituality are all about: finding God and our eternal destiny above and beyond the prison of fleeting time and suffering? Don't we all long to be grasped by the infinite, the absolute, the perfect – to gaze upon

Fra Angelico, *The Annunciation*, ca. 1443

the true, the good, the beautiful, unhindered in peace and glory?

We may indeed ache for paradise. But the gospel, the good news in Christ, is that God lives somewhere else. The true and living God, the one in whom we live and move and have our being, dwells and reigns in the dark depths of our existence, here and now.

The greatness of God's majesty is not in the realm of the eternal. God is Immanuel, "God with us," and even more: he is one of us! The Word became flesh, and in the flesh God's glory is revealed (John 1:14). Such glory, in its incomprehensible smallness, is too much for us to handle. As the apostle John writes, his own neither recognized nor received him.

No wonder we so readily exchange the mystery of incarnation for Christmas. We pine for the familiar rituals of Yuletide merriment and for its visions of confected magic, despite knowing deep down that these are based on a fiction. We want to be comforted and cheered, not scandalized like Joseph or shocked like Mary, the shepherds, and Herod. We don't want to feel, as Bonhoeffer put it, "the shiver of fear that God's coming should arouse in us."

When we sidestep the incarnation, we risk smothering our sense of who God is. We miss, in the words of J. B. Phillips, "the awe-inspiring humility of God" – "the awe, almost a sense of fright, at what God has done."

And what has God done? "He made himself nothing," Paul says (Phil. 2:7 NIV). God has

Fritz von Uhde, *Holy Night,* 1911

dived all the way down into his fallen creation to redeem it, exploding our preconceived notions of the divine. He descended into our darkness, not to shine a glint of light here and there, but to wholly illumine and transform our fleshly existence. He takes on our sinful flesh to overcome it (Heb. 2:14–18).

This is frightening. The One in whom "all things hold together" (Col. 1:17) made himself vulnerable and threw himself into the arms of his wayward creation in order to save it. He came to show us that what we desire and need most is not carefree, self-sufficient lives, but rather a way of humble love.

The day my father pulled me aside into his den and told me that my fifteen-year-old sister had left home to live somewhere else – that was the day I was awakened to my father's love. Up to that point, Dad had been bigger than life. He had everything in control, and he had all the answers. But as he struggled to tell me why my younger sister had left, how she had shattered every trust, his eyes filled with tears of helplessness. At that moment, for the first time, Dad entered my world – my confusing, bewildering, charged world of adolescence. And for the very first time I knew my father's love, not just for me, but for all of us in the family. He and I – we were now the same! I saw then, as I hadn't seen before, the man in him. And I was changed. In confiding his pain to me I too had become a man, through being overwhelmed by love.

Our world does not appreciate vulnerability. Neediness is rejected as incompetence, kindness is dismissed as unprofitable. We want a God who is almighty and invincible, a God who destroys evil in a flash and makes everything all right with a wave of his hand. We want a God who wakes us from our nightmares and transports us into a trouble-free world.

And so God's humility is not only frightening; it is also offensive. We prefer the kind of God we can soar up to and glory in. We don't want to admit that our efforts to reach him are not only futile, but unworthy. God's descent means we cannot come up to him; it is he who comes down to us! He alone bridges the gulf between what is and what ought to be, and shows us this not in a display of power, but by the embarrassing journey of climbing down.

We not only resist God's beggarly ways, but also prefer to ignore them in our everyday lives. The wisdom of our world extols success, financial independence, and status. The good life, we are told, is about having it all together, moving up, being in first place, being head and shoulders above the pack. To know God, however, means the very opposite. We are to have "the mind of Christ" (Phil. 2:5), which means being willing to move down with him.

To know the incarnate God means seeing ourselves for who we really are: trapped in sin and encased in the lonely castles built of our own pride. It means confessing our own complicity in the hells we find ourselves in and have made on earth. And more than this, it means spending ourselves on behalf of the poor, those who exist on the margins of society and at the end of their rope. It means forgoing the security of our lives, and entering into the pain of those who despair. "'Is this not what it means to know me,' declares the Lord, 'to defend the cause of the poor and the needy?'" (Jer. 22:16).

The incarnation, from the manger to the cross, is the very opposite of our wishes. It defies our logic and exposes our self-righteousness and bankruptcy. It reveals how obsessed we are with ourselves. We know in our bones that our rightful end is hell, banishment from the Garden. But the good news is that this is precisely where God meets us. God dwells in the godforsaken places of our lives. His aim is to vanquish every hell, not by external force of will but from the inside out, through love.

Divine depths. Downward. In this lies our hope. "When God's time comes," says Christoph Blumhardt, "great changes take place. Not only are the shepherds of this world

Rembrandt Harmenszoon van Rijn, *The Adoration of the Magi,* 1632

startled, but the whole world – then we are led into something new."

Wherever and whoever we are, no matter what the hell we find ourselves in, Christ descends to us, and calls us to descend with him. On this downward way, we will discover not just the depth of God's love, but also – in the same moment – its divine height.

Balázs Boda, *Floating*, 2003

The Weapons of Grace

An Interview with Philip Yancey

It's almost four decades since he first addressed the problem of pain in his 1977 book Where Is God When It Hurts? *Since then, Philip Yancey has authored or coauthored a string of books on faith and doubt that are widely regarded as classics, including three with physician Paul Brand* (Fearfully and Wonderfully Made, In His Image, *and* Pain: The Gift Nobody Wants).

Yet despite a long public career, the author has written surprisingly little about his own story. Who is the Yancey we never knew? Plough editor Charles E. Moore decided to ask him.

Plough: Your books address questions that most people prefer to avoid – pain, grief, and loss. Yet your books have been bestsellers. Why?

Philip Yancey: The Book of Ecclesiastes includes a striking phrase, "eternity in our hearts." No matter how distracting and entertaining our culture tries to be, questions about meaning,

about life and death, somehow edge their way in. Moments of national crisis bring them to the surface, as well as smaller, more intimate moments. I've had some of my most profound conversations in the waiting room of a hospice or ICU ward with people whose names I don't even know.

Have you struggled personally with the question of suffering?

Mainly, I struggle with the unfairness of suffering. I just wrote a letter to a couple whose child fought valiantly against genetic defects requiring dozens of surgeries, only to succumb to an HIV-contaminated blood transfusion. How do you explain these things? You can't.

Suffering is not a mathematical puzzle. It's desperate human need. We should respond not with words but with practical acts of love and compassion. Remember Job's three friends? They tore their clothes and sat with Job in silence for seven days and seven nights. That was true friendship. The problems started when they opened their mouths.

As a journalist I've traveled the world, interviewing hundreds of people. Some are famous and wildly successful, while others live in poverty and are seemingly cursed by suffering. Life is unfair – so much depends on accidents of birth, or DNA, or family background.

I've found that those who face failure and suffering are more likely to develop a nourishing faith than those who know success and pleasure. Fertilizer stinks, but it helps things grow.

Like Job, you've admitted to having doubts. How have you remained a Christian despite these doubts?

Doubts can be healthy. I'm a Christian because I came to doubt some of what my childhood church taught me, such as the inferiority of other races and of women. When I speak on college campuses, I challenge the skeptics to find a single argument against God voiced by the New Atheists such as Christopher Hitchens and Richard Dawkins, or the Old Atheists such as Bertrand Russell and Voltaire, that is not voiced in biblical books such as Job, Ecclesiastes, Psalms, Lamentations, or Habakkuk. God not only allows us to doubt but provides the very words we can use.

Some of the skeptics are skilled at poking holes in the Bible, but if you take their own assumptions and push them further, it gets sticky. How should we live if we believe that humanity is the product of random forces, with a short life that ends in oblivion? We should doubt our doubts as well as doubt our faith.

You have written that "we all need trustworthy doubt companions." Who are yours?

For a time I participated in a small group of couples who were involved in high-profile Christian ministry. All of us had experienced difficulties expressing honest doubt and temptation in a local church setting. We formed a safe place to talk about those matters – and believe me, high-profile Christians have no exemption when it comes to doubt.

We should doubt our doubts as well as doubt our faith.

In the end, though, I think my readers are my true doubt companions. Many write to me and say something like, "I thought I was the only one." Well, I feel that way too. I put my struggles out there in print, sometimes with fear and trembling, and then learn that I'm just articulating something that others have experienced.

I should add that we need "faith companions" as well as "doubt companions": friends who don't punish us for doubting, but hold on and show us light in the midst of our darkness.

You broke your neck in a car accident in 2007; you've said that the accident changed you spiritually. How?

While recovering, I became aware of how few people were on my "love" list. I had emerged from a repressive church and family and was guarded and bristling with defense mechanisms. I had to pray for love. God in his mercy is beginning to answer that prayer. I have a few long-term close friendships, a rather small blood family, and some adults who have been dear mentors to me.

Often I've asked people, "When did you grow most spiritually?" Almost never will someone mention an easy time when all went well. They'll describe an ICU ward when their daughter's life hung in the balance, or a bankruptcy, or a grueling mission trip.

The accident in 2007 took away my fear of death. I lay on that backboard reflecting that the God I have come to know and love is a God of grace and mercy, a trustworthy God.

Jesus showed a way of grace, not of fuzzy tolerance.

The accident also was a hallmark event for my marriage. We had been coasting along, avoiding emotional land mines and resigned to living with certain recurring problems. The near-death experience put everything in a new perspective. Those problems we had were nothing compared to what we would face if I had ended up as a quadriplegic. Overnight, mountains shrank into molehills and our marriage grew stronger.

What has kept you and your wife Janet together for forty-five years, despite these tensions?

I should probably give you a spiritual answer, but the most honest answer is sheer stubbornness. We have very different personalities, which presents its own challenges. Also, we're both control freaks, convinced our way is the best. It took us years to learn to operate as a team, rather than as rivals. When we travel, especially overseas, those different personalities truly complement each other. Janet is an extrovert, engaging with our hosts, while I'm trying to figure out what to say at a speaking event I've just learned about.

We both entered marriage with wounds: mine from church and family, and Janet's from trying to find her identity as a third-culture missionary kid. I fell madly in love. I thought she did too – only later did I realize that she had adopted me as a kind of social work project. Yet when we said the "till death do us part" vow, we meant it.

You've expressed concern that the church has become an enemy of sinners. But isn't there the opposite danger too – of a fuzzy tolerance that accepts anything and anybody, all in the name of God's unconditional love?

I see a difference in accepting anybody and accepting anything. Jesus pushed the ideals of righteousness higher and higher. You haven't committed adultery; have you lusted? You haven't murdered; have you hated? Be perfect as your Father in heaven is perfect. You can't get any higher than that. His point was that none of us can earn God's acceptance through our behavior.

Jesus did not compromise on the ideals, but he did beautifully describe and embody God's unconditional love for anyone – a leprous beggar, a Samaritan woman with five failed marriages, a traitor like Peter, a human-rights abuser like Saul of Tarsus, a prodigal son. I once plotted on a graph all the people Jesus encountered. The more socially outcast, morally offensive, and disreputable people were, the more attracted they were to Jesus. The more upright, respectable, and even "godly" people were, the more challenged they were by Jesus. They were the ones who had him arrested.

Jesus showed a way of keeping the highest standards while offering Living Water to the least deserving. That's grace, not fuzzy tolerance.

You've pointed out that the church "has always found ways to soften Jesus' strong words on morality." This is precisely the concern that conservative Christians feel today regarding the sexual revolution. Yet you chastise these same Christians for speaking out on morality. Why?

We are fighting battles with evil and injustice – yet, as Martin Luther King Jr. used to say, we fight with different weapons, the weapons of grace. As he said, you can pass laws to force a white man to serve a black man in a restaurant, but you can't pass a law requiring the white man to love the black man. We have higher goals than politics, and you'll never attain those goals through politics alone.

I get concerned when Christians see politics as the answer. Politics is an adversary sport in which you win by slandering your opponent. Jesus showed a different way: Love your enemies, pray for those who persecute you.

The early Christians faced a far more hostile environment in the Roman Empire than we do in the United States today. They set in motion a new community, pioneer settlements of the kingdom of God that could show the world a better way to be human. Tend to the sick, rescue the abandoned babies, free the slaves, love the oppressors, care for the poor – they lived in a new way, and the world took notice.

You believe that the church works best as a "conscience to society that keeps itself at arm's length from the state." The church, in other words, should be a minority counterculture. Isn't that sectarian tribalism?

Quite the contrary. The church was born at Pentecost, a multicultural gathering that had attracted people from many tongues and nations. Unlike Judaism or Islam, the church disengaged from a particular place and culture. The new converts then went back to their own societies to fulfill the Great Commission.

In my travels, I've seen clusters of devout Christians in communist China, in repressive Islamic states, in prisons in Chile and Russia, in Myanmar, and in many other places. Pentecost set the faith loose to adapt to all sorts of environments. In Christ there is neither Jew nor Greek, slave nor free, male nor female, declared Paul – a Pharisee who had probably thanked God daily that he was born Jewish, free, and male, until he encountered the liberating power of the gospel.

"Sectarian tribalism" may be a natural human tendency, but it's one area where the church needs to show a different way, an unnatural way.

What does this unnatural way look like?

I study Jesus and Paul in vain if I'm looking for a way to "change the world." Surely they were aware of the great societal evils around them – think of Romans paying to watch gladiators murder each other for sport – but they gave us no global formula. Instead, they called Christians to show the world a different way to live, to become pioneer settlers of the kingdom of God. Against all odds, that eventually prevailed in Rome. People saw that the Christians freed slaves (some of them), treated women with dignity, nursed plague victims rather than fleeing, and adopted abandoned babies.

I don't have much hope on a global scale, but on a cosmic scale I believe God will intervene rather dramatically when Jesus returns. In the meantime, my hope rests in small groups of Christians around the world showing what God had in mind. In his recent book *The Church in Exile,* Lee Beach describes the church in a phrase I like: "communities of engaged nonconformity." It's up to us to show the world a different way. ⤳

Interview by Charles E. Moore.

Three Questions

Leo Tolstoy

Illustrated by Phillip Gneiting

I T ONCE OCCURRED TO A CERTAIN KING that if he always knew the right time to begin everything; if he knew who were the right people to listen to, and whom to avoid; and, above all, if he always knew what was the most important thing to do, he would never fail in anything he might undertake.

And this thought having occurred to him, he had it proclaimed throughout his kingdom that he would give a great reward to anyone who would teach him what was the right time for every action, and who were the most necessary people, and how he might know what was the most important thing to do.

And learned men came to the king, but they all answered his questions differently.

In reply to the first question, some said that to know the right time for every action, one must draw up in advance a table of days, months, and years, and must live strictly according to it. Only thus, said they, could everything be done at its proper time. Others declared that it was impossible to decide beforehand the right time for every action, but that, not letting oneself be absorbed in idle pastimes, one should always attend to all that was going on, and then do what was most needful. Others, again, said that however attentive the king might be to what was going on, it was impossible for one man to decide correctly the right time for every action, but that he should have a council of wise men who would help him to fix the proper time for everything.

But then again others said there were some things which could not wait to be laid before a council, but about which one had at once to decide whether to undertake them or not. But in order to decide that, one must know beforehand what was going to happen. It is only magicians who know that; and, therefore, in order to know the right time for every action, one must consult magicians.

Equally various were the answers to the second question. Some said the people the king most needed were his councilors; others, the priests; others, the doctors; while some said the warriors were the most necessary.

To the third question, as to what was the most important occupation, some replied that the most important thing in the world was science. Others said it was skill in warfare; and others, again, that it was religious worship.

This short story, written in 1903, is taken from The Gospel in Tolstoy: Selections from His Short Stories, Spiritual Writings, and Novels *(Plough, 2015). Translated by Louise and Aylmer Maude.*

All the answers being different, the king agreed with none of them, and gave the reward to none. But still wishing to find the right answers to his questions, he decided to consult a hermit, widely renowned for his wisdom.

The hermit lived in a wood which he never quitted, and he received none but common folk. So the king put on simple clothes and, before reaching the hermit's cell, dismounted from his horse. Leaving his bodyguard behind, he went on alone.

When the king approached, the hermit was digging the ground in front of his hut. Seeing the king, he greeted him and went on digging. The hermit was frail and weak, and each time he stuck his spade into the ground and turned a little earth, he breathed heavily.

The king went up to him and said: "I have come to you, wise hermit, to ask you to answer three questions: How can I learn to do the right thing at the right time? Who are the people I most need, and to whom should I, therefore, pay more attention than to the rest? And, what affairs are the most important and need my first attention?"

The hermit listened to the king, but answered nothing. He just spat on his hand and recommenced digging.

"You are tired," said the king, "let me take the spade and work awhile for you."

"Thanks!" said the hermit, and, giving the spade to the king, he sat down on the ground.

When he had dug two beds, the king stopped and repeated his questions. The hermit again gave no answer, but rose, stretched out his hand for the spade, and said:

"Now rest awhile – and let me work a bit."

But the king did not give him the spade, and continued to dig. One hour passed, and another. The sun began to sink behind the trees, and the king at last stuck the spade into the ground, and said:

"I came to you, wise man, for an answer to my questions. If you can give me none, tell me so, and I will return home."

"Here comes someone running," said the hermit. "Let us see who it is."

The king turned round and saw a bearded man come running out of the wood. The man held his hands pressed against his stomach, and blood was flowing from under them. When he reached the king, he fell fainting on the ground, moaning feebly. The king and the hermit unfastened the man's clothing. There was a large wound in his stomach. The king washed it as best he could, and bandaged it with his handkerchief and with a towel the hermit had. But the blood would not stop flowing, and the king again and again removed the bandage soaked with warm blood, and washed and re-bandaged the wound. When at last the blood ceased flowing, the man revived and asked for something to drink. The king brought fresh water and gave it to him. Meanwhile the sun had set, and it had become cool. So the king, with the hermit's help, carried the wounded man into the hut and laid him on the bed. Lying on the bed, the man closed his eyes and was quiet; but the king was so tired from his walk and from the work he had done that he crouched down on the threshold, and also fell asleep – so soundly that he slept all through the short summer night. When he awoke in the morning, it was long before he could remember where he was, or who was the strange bearded man lying on the bed and gazing intently at him with shining eyes.

"Forgive me!" said the bearded man in a weak voice, when he saw that the king was awake and was looking at him.

"I do not know you, and have nothing to forgive you for," said the king.

"You do not know me, but I know you. I am that enemy of yours who swore to revenge himself on you, because you executed his brother and seized his property. I knew you had gone alone to see the hermit, and I resolved to kill you on your way back. But the day passed and you did not return. So I came out from my ambush to find you, and came upon your bodyguard, and they recognized me, and wounded me. I escaped from them, but should have bled to death had you not dressed my wound. I wished to kill you, and you have saved my life. Now, if I live, and if you wish it, I will serve you as your most faithful slave, and will bid my sons do the same. Forgive me!"

The king was very glad to have made peace with his enemy so easily, and to have gained him for a friend, and he not only forgave him, but said he would send his servants and his own physician to attend him, and promised to restore his property.

Having taken leave of the wounded man, the king went out into the porch and looked around for the hermit. Before going away he wished once more to beg an answer to the questions he had put. The hermit was outside, on his knees, sowing seeds in the beds that had been dug the day before.

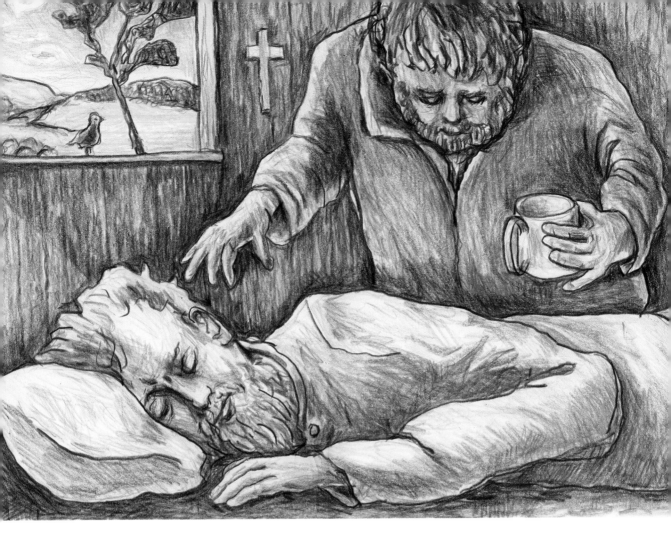

The king approached him and said, "For the last time, I pray you to answer my questions, wise man."

"You have already been answered!" said the hermit, still crouching on his thin legs, and looking up at the king, who stood before him.

"How answered? What do you mean?" asked the king.

"Do you not see?" replied the hermit. "If you had not pitied my weakness yesterday, and had not dug these beds for me, but had gone your way, that man would have attacked you, and you would have repented of not having stayed with me. So the most important time was when you were digging the beds; and I was the most important man; and to do me good was your most important business. Afterwards, when that man ran to us, the most important time was when you were attending to him, for if you had not bound up his wounds he would have died without having made peace with you. So he was the most important man, and what you did for him was your most important business. Remember then: there is only one time that is important – now! It is the most important time because it is the only time when we have any power. The most necessary person is the one with whom you are, for no man knows whether he will ever have dealings with anyone else: and the most important affair is to do that person good, because for that purpose alone was man sent into this life." ⤳

IN SEARCH OF ROBERT LAX

Bard of God's Circus

TIMOTHY J. KEIDERLING

THE NEW YORK TIMES praised his 1959 work *Circus of the Sun* as "perhaps the greatest English-language poem of this century." A reckless claim, perhaps, yet still today the minimalist poet Robert Lax (1915–2000) has his devotees, especially among fans of Thomas Merton, with whom he shared a lifelong friendship. Because of the hidden quality of his life, however, he is not as widely known as his contemporaries and friends such as Jack Kerouac or Merton himself.

With any luck, Michael McGregor's compelling new biography will help change that. In telling Lax's story, he's been aided by the subject himself, who kept voluminous journals throughout his life, sometimes writing thirty to forty pages a day. Using these entries, McGregor recreates conversations and scenes that are as vivid as a screenplay.

Lax's work and life, McGregor argues, can best be understood in terms of what he, borrowing from Aquinas, called "pure act" – a life of simplicity, poverty, and joy, lived completely in the moment. In the words of one of Lax's poems, quoted by McGregor as a kind of manifesto:

there are not many songs
there is only one song

the animals lope to it
the fish swim to it
the sun circles to it
the stars rise
the snow falls
the grass grows

there is no end to the song and no beginning
the singer may die
but the song is forever

truth is the name of the song
and the song is truth.

Born to a New York Jewish family, Lax first met Merton at Columbia University, where both worked at the *Jester,* a student humor magazine. Both would go on to join the staff of the *Columbia Review,* with Lax as editor-in-chief. In the evenings, he and Merton would go listen to jazz musicians, and Lax later remembered the musicians' free yet unified playing as his first experience of "pure act."

The year 1943 marked a decisive turn: Lax followed Merton's lead and converted to Catholicism – a decision inspired in part by reading Catholic writers such as Aquinas,

Pure Act: The Uncommon Life of Robert Lax
Michael N. McGregor
(Fordham)

Untitled poem in Robert Lax's *Journal C* (Pendo, 1990)

Dante, and (not least) James Joyce, whose run-on style he imitated in his journals. According to Ed Rice, who served as godfather to both new converts, Lax "was born a Catholic and finally got baptized," unlike Merton, who "really had to struggle with it." Though Merton's entry into the Trappist order meant an outward separation, the two corresponded faithfully.

As an aspiring writer, Lax initially met only discouragement, flitting from one job to the next, first on the staff of the *New Yorker* and then as *Time's* poetry editor. Though often despondent over his failure to find a publisher, he worried about the danger of "committing suicide" as a poet by abandoning his voice in order to find a readership. Through this search for genuineness, he met the Cristiani family, who owned a circus, and spent months traveling with them. To Lax, the artistry of the circus reflected the creativity of God, the maker of the universe and master of history. These experiences served as material for *Circus of the Sun,* his best-known book, which portrays all life as taking place under a heavenly gaze:

Who is it for whom we now perform,
Cavorting on wire:
For whom does the boy
Climbing the ladder
Balance and whirl –
For whom,
Seen or unseen
In a shield of light?

The beginning of the 1950s found Lax in Marseilles. Life in southern France was a revelation, a manifestation of the same genuine "pure act" that he had seen in the Cristiani circus: "The great thing in Marseille is not the buildings; it is the people . . . All who live here walk the decks of their city with grace and equilibrium, the joy of acrobats and sailors." He would spend much of the next two years in France, working in Paris at a literary magazine alongside Jack Kerouac, whose work he came to champion.

Lax's search for a place to live that was quiet, warm, and cheap led him in November 1968 to the Greek island of Kalymnos (he'd already been living in Greece off and on since 1961). Soon after arriving, he received a letter from Merton proposing a reunion – the first for the two friends in years. They planned to meet on the top of Mount Athos, the "Holy Mountain" of Eastern Orthodox monasticism. It was not to be. On December 11, Lax received a telegram informing him that Merton had been electrocuted by a badly wired appliance while attending a conference in Bangkok.

Shocked by his friend's death, Lax retreated into a life of quiet: "Thinking somehow day and night about him . . . Glad to be here where every part of the landscape makes sense." He determined to stay on Kalymnos, retreating to Patmos during seasons when tourists swarmed the larger island.

Paradoxically, it was in these years that Lax's work finally began to receive international attention. The BBC broadcast a forty-minute reading of his poems, and several notable writers including British critic R. C. Kenedy published appreciative studies. For Lax, such recognition, so long withheld, was immensely gratifying.

Patmos, the island on which John wrote the Book of Revelation, is where McGregor met Lax in 1985. Lax understood the younger man's quest for a genuine way of living, and McGregor in turn was deeply impressed by the poet's quiet simplicity and joy. This biography is a sensitive testimony to their subsequent fifteen years of friendship, and to the "pure act" that Lax knew to be at the heart of life as God intended it. ⤳

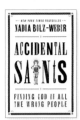

Accidental Saints: Finding God in All the Wrong People
Nadia Bolz-Weber
(Convergent Books)

Bolz-Weber, a Lutheran pastor, cares about people. That care shines through her book, in which she offers herself and her eclectic parishioners as evidence that Jesus indeed came for outcasts and misfits. A former alcoholic, she knows firsthand that "the power of unbounded mercy, of what we call The Gospel, cannot be destroyed by corruption and toothy TV preachers. Because in the end, there is still Jesus." This Jesus loves everyone – addicts, teenage girls who cut themselves, overweight middle-aged white people, NRA enthusiasts, and Adam Lanza. She writes convincingly about taking part in a community in which repentance, confession, and absolution are real. (Read an excerpt at *plough.com/bolz-weber*.) And she leaves us with a challenge: do our lives and churches and friendships, in their breadth and boldness, bear witness to Jesus' unconditional love for every person?

Yet Bolz-Weber gets crucial things wrong. Not the tattoos, snark, and casual expletives that have, by design or not, made her a poster-pastor for hipster Christianity. The deeper problem is that, despite the countercultural packaging, her book actually sidesteps much of what's truly subversive about Jesus' good news – specifically, his challenge to "keep my commandments" and "take up your cross and follow me." She hates it, she says, when Christianity gets sentimental. Yet isn't that what's happening when talk of freedom isn't paired with a call to discipleship, or when, for example, she says she's willing to marry Jim and Stuart? Too often, she ends up with an unthreatening, self-indulgent gospel that plays all too well in today's culture.

Despite these blind spots, *Accidental Saints* is a colorful reminder that, as Jesus promised, we'll all be surprised at the sort of people entering the kingdom before us.

$2.00 a Day: Living on Almost Nothing in America
Kathryn J. Edin and
H. Luke Shaefer
(Houghton Mifflin Harcourt)

In 1996, with one stroke of the pen, President Clinton did away with Aid to Families with Dependent Children, effectively ending welfare as we knew it. Daniel Patrick Moynihan, then a US senator, had predicted that this would result in "children sleeping on grates, picked up in the morning frozen." Dramatic words – but, as *$2.00 a Day* reveals, they are uncomfortably close to the truth, with 1.5 million American households, including three million children, now living below the two-bucks-a-day benchmark of extreme poverty.

In the course of twenty years studying poverty, Edin began to notice just how many people were slipping through the safety net of government aid. In this book, she documents the desperate survival strategies of families in Chicago, Cleveland, Mississippi, and rural Appalachia who live a virtually cashless life, ineligible for, or unaware of, the emergency aid that is available.

To take one example: after her marriage fell apart, Modonna, a high school graduate with two years of college, could only find a job as a cashier. She and her daughter were able to rent a one-room apartment and just get by. Then one day Modonna's register came up $10 short and she was fired on the spot. The missing cash was later found, but Modonna wasn't re-hired. Soon she and her daughter were homeless, going from shelter to shelter while she tried again and again for a job. (One thing people in this book have in common: they want to work but can't find or keep a job.)

At the end of their book, Edin and Shaefer offer practical suggestions for stopping this cycle of poverty. Let's hope that enough of us are shocked and outraged by what they describe to take action. ➤ *The Editors*

Painting by Rosemary Millette, Wild Wings, www.artbarbarians.com

STEVEN KNEPPER

Rediscovering Wonder

Upon its publication in June 2015, Pope Francis's encyclical *Laudato si'* drew predictably opposing reactions. For both fans and critics, the key term was "climate change." Whether in the form of plaudits from the left or groans from the right, there seemed to be wide consensus that the central purpose of *Laudato si'* was to call for reducing carbon emissions, with a few redistributionist flourishes thrown in for good measure.

Climate change is undoubtedly a crucial issue to Francis. Yet at the encyclical's heart are concerns that challenge both sides of the partisan debate.

One such concern is the Pope's call for recovering a sense of wonder. Through wonder, says Francis, we can learn to see the true value of "our common home," the world in which we live and upon which we depend. "If we approach nature and the environment

Writings discussed in this essay:

Laudato si' *Encyclical Letter on Care for Our Common Home* Pope Francis, published 2015 at *www.vatican.va*

The Sense of Wonder Rachel Carson *Harper and Row, 1965*

without this openness to awe and wonder," he writes, "if we no longer speak the language of fraternity and beauty in our relationship with the world, our attitude will be that of masters, consumers, ruthless exploiters, unable to set limits on their immediate needs." The encyclical certainly calls for thoughtful, far-seeing policy, but it also suggests that change will depend on grassroots spiritual renewal – on fostering an openness to wonder in our own lives and communities.

We often associate wonder with childhood, and perhaps for Francis, cultivating wonder is one way in which we can "become as little children." My own daughter, now two and a half years old, has certainly helped me rekindle a sense of wonder. The storm clouds billowing up over the mountains, the spider webs glistening with dew in our garden, the fireflies flickering in the gathering night, the

Steven Knepper teaches English at the Virginia Military Institute.

mockingbird's song – her delight in these things has heightened my own.

But wondering children need sympathetic adults. Rachel Carson reflects on this in her 1965 work *The Sense of Wonder,* which describes introducing her young nephew to the Maine woods and seashores. Carson writes: "If a child is to keep alive his inborn sense of wonder, he needs the companionship of at least one adult who can share it, rediscovering with him the joy, excitement, and mystery of the world we live in." This may be even truer today, more than half a century after Carson wrote these words. A child's sense of wonder has probably always been fragile, easily fading with the transition into adulthood. But contemporary Western culture, with its pervasive consumerism, irony, and digital mediation, can be particularly inhospitable to it.

Looking back on my own childhood, I realize I was fortunate to have a number of sure guides to experiencing wonder. I grew up on a small dairy farm in central Pennsylvania. It was no straightforward idyll. A child growing up on a working farm learns early about death and suffering – the stillborn calf, the crops withered by drought, the fawn caught in a haybine. (A child's experience of wonder is often accompanied by an awareness of the terrible.) All the same, there were pastures and woods to explore, I had meaningful work, and I was part of a warm community. My father taught me how to care for our cattle and how to sit patiently in the woods; my mother, how to garden and bird watch; a teenage neighbor, how to find crayfish under rocks in the stream and snakes under rocks in the woods. I had a remarkable teacher for two years in grade school who had us plant trees on the edge of the playground and vegetable seeds on our classroom windowsill. In Boy Scouts I camped and backpacked regularly in Pennsylvania's many state parks.

I also had an older cousin named Tom, a skilled woodsman who took me on many adventures. In the spring we would wade through a sea of May apples, hunting for mushrooms. He taught me to identify trees, since morels tend to grow around ash trees. As evening descended we would listen for wild turkeys flying up to roost, and Tom would hoot like an owl to see if he could get them to gobble. Once, he took me up a steep hollow at twilight to watch a huge colony of bats fly out into a meadow to feed on insects. (The bats have since been devastated by white-nose syndrome, while the ash trees have succumbed to the emerald ash borer – a reminder that wonder can be destroyed not just by inner factors but also by external ones, and with more finality.)

I didn't fully appreciate these childhood guides until I had a daughter of my own and began trying, often not as skillfully, to recreate some of their lessons for her. Carson notes that many adults who want to kindle wonder in children are daunted by the task. They worry that they don't know enough about their local ecosystems – about the bugs, birds, and animals, about the trees and flowers, about the rocks and fossils – to guide a question-asking child. Few of us, after all, are nature sages like Carson (or my cousin Tom, for that matter). But she says that "for the child, and for the parent seeking to guide him, it is not half so important to know as to feel." What children primarily need is someone to wonder with them.

Indeed, to treat their wonder as only a matter of factual questions to be answered may only serve to limit it. According to Aristotle, wonder accompanies our questions about the world and ceases as we find the answers. It is productive – a curiosity or bafflement that spurs our thinking – but it should ultimately be overcome. There is something commonsensical about this. It describes a learning process that we have probably all experienced, in which initial curiosity is eventually sated by inquiry and discovery. It is unsurprising that this has been one of the dominant ways of thinking about wonder in Western history.

But Aristotle's teacher Plato described a different possibility, one that has influenced Christian reflection on the glory of creation. It is openness to this sort of wonder that Pope Francis calls for in *Laudato si'*. Plato held that the world is inexhaustibly wondrous, since it provides apprehensions of the ideal forms. This wonder does not point to a fillable knowledge gap but to the irreducible mystery that there is something rather than nothing, a mystery that ultimately renders all existence uncanny. It often catches us unawares – we walk past the same maple dozens of time without even looking at it until its fiery red foliage arrests us one October day – but we can cultivate openness to it. It raises the largest theological and philosophical questions about the universe, but it also helps us to see even the small and familiar with new eyes. As Kathleen Raine, the twentieth-century Platonist, puts it in her poem "Soliloquies":

> Incredible that anything exists – this hotchpotch
> World of marvels and trivia, and which is which?

If some strands of Platonism have denigrated the material world, Raine's lines point to other possibilities. We see an example of this in children. They are certainly hungry for knowledge, but they have not lost their sense of wonder or been numbed to the strangeness of existence.

These two sorts of wonder are not rigidly opposed; inquiry does not necessarily dissipate wonder. Learning about, say, the symbiotic relationship between honey bees and flowering plants can actually heighten our awe. Carson claims that "if facts are the seeds that later produce knowledge and wisdom, then the emotions and the impressions of the senses are the fertile soil in which the seeds must grow." Many scientists and naturalists, like Carson herself, not only have been led to the microscope by a sense of wonder, but also have wondered at what they discovered there.

Still, as Carson's metaphor for wonder as "fertile soil" suggests, facts alone are sterile. "It is possible to compile extensive lists of creatures seen and identified without once having caught a breath-taking glimpse of the wonder of life," she cautions. To squelch wonder in this way is to lose a source of great experiential depth and resonance, and it can also lead to a dangerous attitude toward nature. The quest for knowledge can easily give way to a hunger for mastery and domination. A nature shorn of wonder can easily become a nature shorn of all value except utility. This has too often been the case in modernity, as the combination of reductive science and a reductive economics have reframed how we see the world, reducing it to exploitable resources.

There is much at stake in our attitudes toward wonder. In fostering wonder, we also cultivate gratitude, reverence, and care. Wendell Berry captures this truth memorably in his poem "The Mad Farmer Manifesto":

> To be sane in a mad time
> is bad for the brain, worse
> for the heart. The world
> is a holy vision, had we clarity
> to see it – a clarity that men
> depend on men to make.

It can often feel like our cultural grasp of this vision is blurry at best. Instead of despairing, though, perhaps we should carry a child outside to look up at the stars. That seemingly trivial gesture may be what we need, as Pope Francis suggests in *Laudato si'*, to see the world clearly for what it is – as God's holy handiwork, to be approached gratefully and with awe. ⇁

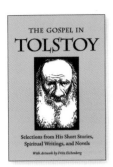

Finding the Good News in Great Literature

The next installment in an ongoing series from Plough, this anthology vividly reveals Tolstoy's lifelong fascination with the life and teachings of Jesus – as none of his novels, novellas, short stories, plays, or essays could on its own. In the hands of a master storyteller, the gospel themes come to life: betrayal and forgiveness, sacrifice and redemption, death and resurrection.

Hailed as one of the world's greatest writers – by the likes of Dostoyevsky, Chekhov, Woolf, Joyce, Proust, Faulkner, and Nabokov – Leo Tolstoy (1828–1910) is best known for his novels *War and Peace* and *Anna Karenina*. But his short stories express a hard-won faith, and his essays on Christianity, nonviolence, and justice profoundly influenced Martin Luther King Jr. and Mahatma Gandhi. Born into Russian nobility, Tolstoy eventually renounced his wealth and title to put his beliefs into practice.

Tolstoy enthusiasts will be pleased to find some of his deepest, most compelling passages in one volume, while new readers will find their appetites whetted for more (see sample story on page 55).

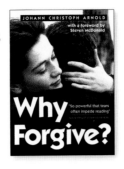

Is Forgiveness for Everyone?

Carol's husband committed adultery. Hashim was shot on a street corner and paralyzed for life. Delf backed a truck over his one-year-old son. Josef escaped the Holocaust. Kate was abused by her alcoholic mother. Bill's son was killed by a drunk driver. Marietta's daughter was kidnapped and murdered. Tragedy struck them all full force, but they refused to remain its victims.

In *Why Forgive?*, one of Plough's all-time bestsellers, Johann Christoph Arnold lets the untidy experiences of ordinary people speak for themselves – people who have earned the right to talk about forgiving. Some of these stories deal with violent crime, betrayal, abuse, bigotry, gang warfare, and genocide. Others address everyday wounds caused by backbiting, conflict in the home, and tensions in the workplace. The book also tackles what can be the biggest challenge: forgiving oneself. These people, who have overcome the cancer of bitterness and hatred, are now helping others unleash the healing power of forgiveness (see interview on page 28).

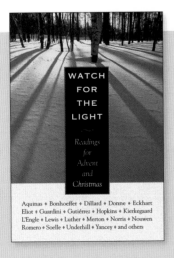

Christmas and Easter are not shopping seasons.

How, in the holiday bustle, can we keep our eyes on Jesus and why he came? These Advent and Lenten readers, with stirring daily reflections from a broad array of Christian writers, can help you start (or end) each day pointed in the right direction.

Allan Rohan Crite, *School's Out*, 1936

Educating *for the* Kingdom

GERHARD CARDINAL MÜLLER

An Address to High School Students and Staff

I have been asked to talk to you about two themes: the kingdom of God, and the importance of education. My first instinct was to talk about how you should put your education at the service of the kingdom, and that is certainly true. But it occurs to me that if we first try to think about what the kingdom of God actually is, the connection we discover between the two themes will throw light on the true dignity and importance of what you are doing as both teachers and students.

What then is the kingdom of God? When we think of a kingdom we think first of a king and then perhaps imagine a certain territory ruled by that king. We may also think of a certain way of organizing that territory or of the laws governing the relationships between the people living there. In other words, we think of the kingdom of God as a place or as a particular political system. Certainly many of the people who first heard Jesus speak would have thought like this.

But it would be wrong to try to reduce the kingdom of God in this way. Even if the place or political system we have in mind were particularly just and peaceful, still the kingdom of God means more than that. Nowhere in the Gospels does Jesus offer an absolutely clear definition of the kingdom. Usually Jesus tells parables about the kingdom and of course parables can have multiple meanings.

Why does the Lord do this? Perhaps because the kingdom of God is bigger and wider and deeper than any human definition can ever fully capture. In the original Greek of the New Testament, the phrase meaning the kingdom of God is: *basileia tou theou.* The word *basileia* is derived from the word *basileus* meaning "the king." A very literal rendering of the word *basileia* would be "that which belongs to, or pertains to the king." That might denote, as the dictionary says, "a political or territorial unit ruled by a king or queen." But we can also think of this thing that belongs to the king less in terms of a place and more in terms of the power and authority which the king possesses.

In one of my academic books, I wrote that the kingdom of God is the "self-communication of God as salvation and life." God himself is present as the kingdom of God: where God rules and we are obedient to God and we accept the fellowship of Jesus, there is the kingdom of God.

The kingdom of God is God's power and authority – giving life to us, which of course entails God being present to us. Perhaps, as Bruderhof pastor J. Heinrich Arnold puts it in his book *Discipleship,* we should say: "Jesus is the kingdom of God in his person. When he forgave sins – that was the kingdom of God. When he gathered his friends in unity – that was the kingdom of God. When he drove out demons and impure spirits – that was the kingdom of God. Every deed of his mission among men was the kingdom of God."

I like both these definitions because they leave open the possibility of saying more. The kingdom of God is Jesus, or God's self-communication – his presence – among us. Yet because God is infinite, anything we say to try to define the kingdom, even if it is true and meaningful will be inadequate, since we cannot set a limit on God.

The New Testament teaches us that in talking of the kingdom of God, we must not lock ourselves in but must open ourselves to a greater reality. In Luke's Gospel Jesus tells us: "Behold, the kingdom of God is in your midst." Yet in the Gospel of John at his trial, Jesus tells Pilate: "My kingdom is not of the world." The kingdom of God, then, is present in the world and must therefore exercise transformative influence on our civil structures and institutions – yet at the same time, it is not of this world, and cannot therefore be exhaustively captured by these structures.

The kingdom of God is both a gift and something we must strive after. In Luke's Gospel, the Lord exhorts us to seek the kingdom of God above all else. So he wishes us to engage our efforts and talents, but then he adds, "and he [God] will give you everything you need." In seeking and striving, we will receive as gifts those things which we need for our personal or social life.

This paradox of the unearned gift, which

In September 2015, Cardinal Müller, the Vatican's prefect of the Congregation for the Doctrine of the Faith, addressed students at the Mount Academy, a high school in upstate New York founded by the Bruderhof, the community that publishes Plough. Müller's two-day visit to the Anabaptist community was the first by a leading Vatican prelate – and carried special resonance as a sign of reconciliation between Catholics and heirs of the Radical Reformation. Watch an interview with Cardinal Müller at *plough.com/muller.*

is something to be achieved by the receiver, seems to me to be a perfect image of Christian education. God himself is our educator. Accordingly, Christian education is not a transaction. Teachers do not receive a salary in return for the cold imparting of a certain amount of information or for transmitting a certain set of skills. Rather, education is the entrusting of a gift from one generation to the next. The older generation's accumulated culture, learning, and skills are given as an unearned gift to the younger. But this gift also carries a responsibility: the younger generation must make the gift a reality in their own lives. This, then, is the hallmark of Christian education: it is the giving of a gift that will be made into reality by the one who receives it.

Is this not precisely what the Lord does with the kingdom? "Seek the kingdom of God above all and he will give you everything you need." Can we not say then that the task of educating is in many respects an image of the Lord's kingdom? And can we not go further and say that this task of educating, of receiving an education, is actually a way of participating in the kingdom?

Seen in this light, Christian education is not just a tiresome task, although it may at times have its difficulties. How grateful we should be for this wonderful opportunity! Does it not make us think again of our own dignity? We are not just students, teachers, janitors, secretaries, catering or support staff – we are agents of the Lord's kingdom.

Of course, once we recognize our own dignity, then equally we must also recognize the dignity of souls around us. Shouldn't that have a transformative effect on how we treat our classmates, teachers, and colleagues, since they are our brothers and sisters? If we realize what we are working for, then surely we will realize that only our best efforts are worthy of such a project. Must we not then renew our efforts?

While doing so, however, we must always remember *whose* is the kingdom that we're working for. Often we try to rely entirely on our own efforts, and forget God. We can trust in him because he is never outdone in generosity.

Writing about education, Johann Christoph Arnold has remarked: "Children need time to breathe in and breathe out. They need time to play." This is true also of the children of the kingdom of God. We need time to play. And we take time to pray. It is therefore good and fitting that you take time and moments of prayer, both communally and individually, to offer your day and work to the Lord. You may be sure that if you do this, he will find ways of blessing you – even if it does not always take the form you expect. Saint Paul tells us in the Letter to the Romans, "In all things God works for the good of those who love him."

It seems fitting to conclude with some final words from J. Heinrich Arnold's *Discipleship*:

> What a mighty thing it is to live for God's kingdom! Do not shrink back. Live for it, look for it and you will find it is so powerful it will completely overwhelm you. It will solve every problem on earth. Everything will become new and each person will love the other in Christ. All separation brought about by death will be overcome and love will rule. ⇘

This article is based on a talk given on September 24, 2015 at the Mount Academy in Esopus, New York.

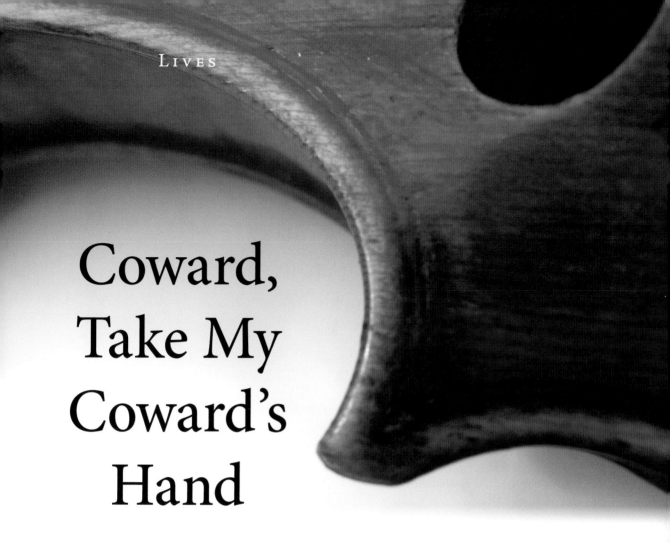

Coward, Take My Coward's Hand

The Brave Legacy of Chris Farlekas

MAUREEN SWINGER

When Chris Spero Farlekas, our neighbor here in New York's Hudson Valley, died on May 5, 2015, his obituary read like three men's lives run together. Among his roles across eighty-six years: army medic in a MASH unit in Korea, civil rights activist, war correspondent in Vietnam, amateur violinist, and philanthropist.

But when his friends gathered to celebrate his life, they had other stories to share – quieter, more painful, and more powerful than the tributes in print.

Chris grew up as the son of Greek immigrants and volunteered for the army in 1949. After boot camp, he shipped off to Korea in 1950 to join the Eleventh Medical Evacuation Hospital Unit.

By his own account, his first taste of combat nearly unhinged him. The enemy struck at night, and his only chance of identifying friend or foe was by the light of tracer fire. He held his ground and tried to reach one buddy, then another. But caught between so many cries for help, he lost his bearings. He sank to his knees and began to dig frantically in the bloody mud. Somewhere, a childhood memory was calling him back. He was maybe six years old, digging in his front yard, and a friendly neighbor was leaning over the fence chortling, "Young man, you dig so deep, you're liable to get to China." Perhaps now the tunnel could reach the other way.

His superior officer stumbled across him and roared at him to get up. "Farlekas, the men need you!" Chris kept digging. The lieutenant dragged him up and slapped him. "Get away!" shouted Chris. "I'm going home!" Then the lieutenant did something that threw Chris's life onto a new track. He carried the young man over to a small tree, leaned him up against the trunk, and above the roar of battle, shouted the words of a poem into his ear.

> Only we two, and yet our howling can
> Encircle the world's end.
> Frightened, you are my only friend.
>
> And frightened, we are everyone.
> Someone must make a stand.
> Coward, take my coward's hand.
> (from Eve Merriam, "The Coward")

Chris would later recall looking in dazed amazement at his superior officer, who had recognized in him a man who had the potential for bravery. On that night, as bullets shredded leaves above his head, he became that someone who must make a stand.

From then on while in Korea, according to fellow soldiers, he took risks that seemed beyond the call of duty. And when there was nothing more to be done for a dying comrade, he found one more thing to do – take down his final words for his family. Sometimes it was forgiveness pleaded, sometimes forgiveness owed. He heard memories of swings in haylofts, moms' Sunday dinners, girls left behind, children that might have been. He kept them

all, scrawled in a journal, to be delivered on his return – if he ever did return. When he closed the book, he held the hand of the man whose words he'd written down, until the man was gone.

Chris came home in 1952 with his journal, his memories, and his medals. In the next years, he followed up on his promises to the boys who didn't return. Altogether he traveled more than fifteen thousand miles around the United States to visit their families and share their messages from the pages of his battered journal. According to Justin Nadal, a friend:

One of his most painful visits centered around a man named Steve Kroll. Steve was his friend in the unit, and one night he was almost torn apart by a grenade. An early dialysis machine was being tested in the MASH unit, and Chris was part of the team that used it to try to keep Steve alive. Steve suffered horribly, and all efforts to save him failed. When he finally died, Chris was ordered to assist in the autopsy. It was part of the protocols set in place to see how and if the machine had

worked. He pleaded to be exempted, but he was refused, and had to watch as the doctor took his friend apart. It was a vision that tortured him up to his own death.

After the war, he most wanted to go to Crivitz, Wisconsin, to meet with the Kroll family. When he arrived at their farmhouse, they treated him like a son. As he had done in so many homes around the country, he sat in their living room and prepared to tell the family about their son's last minutes of life. But this time it was different – he was talking about his own good friend. The pain was deep.

At the end of the visit, Chris asked if he could play his violin in honor of Steve, as a gift to the family. They accepted. Chris played for an hour, tears flowing in remembrance of his friend's life and in mourning for his agonized death. When he finished, he laid his violin gently in its case, closed it and never played the instrument again. Call it a flair for the dramatic, call it a moment of honor, it was how Chris chose to capture the magnitude of the event.

As war correspondent for the *Times Herald-Record,* a regional newspaper, Chris again found himself on the other side of the world, in Vietnam – "in the back of a truck with a bunch of scared young soldiers." For the second time he was on the front, notebook in hand, witnessing friends going into mortal danger, and writing to tell about it – to tell about them.

Writing was one way Chris could keep people from forgetting and from being forgotten. In the Hudson Valley, Chris himself is also remembered for other things: not only his penchant for goofy glasses, his dazzlingly bright cane, and his hot red car, but also for the Thanksgiving pies he baked for families who were low on money and for the red suit he donned at Christmas to deliver presents he'd collected through the year.

Cancer closed in on Chris's later years, and despite his many friends, he often found himself alone. Hounded by all the death he'd seen over the years, the fear sometimes seemed overwhelming. At such times, all he wanted was what he had given to so many others – a hand to hold. "Frightened, you are my only friend. And frightened, we are everyone."

Now Chris is gone. But his legacy – of a hand bravely extended – lives on. ➤

Chris Farlekas backstage after an appearance as Kris Kringle, Christmas 2007

Mother Maria of Paris

JASON LANDSEL

Paris, ca. 1932: "I was walking along the Boulevard Montparnasse and I saw: in front of a café, on the pavement, there was a table, on the table was a glass of beer and behind the glass was sitting a Russian nun in full monastic robes. I looked at her and decided that I would never go near that woman." So Metropolitan Anthony remembered his first encounter with Mother Maria Skobtsova.

Mother Maria was born in 1891 in Riga and christened Elizaveta Pilenko. Her father died while she was still a teenager; this led her to become an atheist. After moving with her mother to St. Petersburg, Russia, she drifted into socialist circles, and at age eighteen married Dmitri Kuzmin-Karaviev, an Old Bolshevik activist. They separated after only three years, shortly before the birth of their first child.

Though soon disillusioned by the endless theorizing of many would-be radicals, Elizaveta, now a recognized poet, never lost her passion for social justice. Gradually, this passion led her back to Jesus, though she still espoused atheism. In Jesus, she saw one who was oppressed and yet who died heroically for others.

In 1917, the Russian Revolution began with fierce fighting between the communist Red Army and the reactionary White Army. Elizaveta, who had served as deputy mayor in a Red town, was captured by the White Army and charged as a revolutionary. Thanks to a compassionate judge, Daniel Skobtsov, she was spared the death penalty. She visited him after the trial to express her thanks; a few days later they married. Fleeing Russia to escape the Bolsheviks, the couple eventually moved to Paris.

In 1926, Elizaveta's young daughter Anastasia died. Keeping watch over her, Elizaveta felt that at last she glimpsed the depths of eternity and the meaning of repentance. She wrote:

> Now I want an authentic and purified road. Not out of faith in life, but in order to justify, understand, and accept death. . . . No amount of thought will ever result in any greater formulation than the three words, "Love one another," so long as it is love to the end and without exceptions. And then the whole of life is illumined, which is otherwise an abomination and a burden.

That year, she separated from her second husband, devoting herself to social work. She took vows as an Orthodox nun six years later, taking the name Maria. Soon the spiritual self-concern of Christians was infuriating her just as much as leftist theorizing had. "Piety, piety," she wrote in her diary, "but where is the love that moves mountains?"

Prompted by that love, she pioneered what she called "monasticism in the world," founding a house of hospitality for homeless women. As the community grew, Mother Maria often reminded her sisters that their calling was simply to "give from the heart," since "each person is the very icon of God incarnate in the world."

After Nazi forces occupied Paris in 1940, Mother Maria joined an underground circle providing false papers for Jewish Parisians. In 1943, she was arrested and sent to the Ravensbrück concentration camp. According to fellow inmates, she would regularly gather the other women for encouragement, often sharing her food rations at the cost of her own health. On Good Friday 1945, she, together with other sick prisoners, was selected for the gas chambers. She died on Holy Saturday, as the guns of the approaching Red Army boomed in the distance. ❧

Jason Landsel is the artist for Plough's *"Forerunners" series, including Mother Maria's portrait opposite. For more about her, see* Mother Maria Skobtsova: Essential Writings, *ed. Jim Forest (Orbis, 2003).*